Jonah who will be 25
in the year 2000

*Jonas qui aura 25 ans
en l'an 2000*

*Jonah who will be 25
in the year 2000*

a film by **Alain Tanner**

screenplay by **John Berger**
and **Alain Tanner**

translated by **Michael Palmer**

*North Atlantic Books
Berkeley, California*

Jonah who will be 25 in the year 2000

English translation

Copyright © 1983, Society for the Study of Native Arts and Sciences
Copyright © 1978, Cinematique Suisse, of original French screenplay
ISBN 0-913028-98-3

Published by North Atlantic Books
2320 Blake Street
Berkeley, California 94704

Book design and graphic production by Paula Morrison
Typeset in Baskerville by Rob Baker, Cort Smith and Barbara Naiditch

Jonah who will be 25 in the year 2000 is a New Yorker Films release
and available from New Yorker Films, 16 West 61st Street, New York,
New York 10023.

Jonah who will be 25 in the year 2000 is sponsored by the Society for the
Study of Native Arts and Sciences, a nonprofit educational corporation
whose goals are to develop an ecological and crosscultural perspective
linking various scientific, social, and artistic fields; to nurture a holistic
view of arts, sciences, humanities, and healing; and to publish and distri-
bute literature on the relationship of mind, body, and nature.

The Society for the Study of Native Arts and Sciences would like to
thank the following people for their help in making this text available:
John Berger and Alain Tanner, for their gracious permission and careful
reading of the translation; Alain Tanner for the copy of the interview with
him and the stills of the film; the Pacific Film Archive of the University
Art Museum, Berkeley, California, for the use of their facilities; and
Daniel Talbot of New Yorker Films in New York for the loan of the film.

First printing

Library of Congress Cataloging in Publication Data

Berger, John.
   Jonah who will be 25 in the year 2000 = Jonas qui aura 25 ans en
l'an 2000.

   Translation of: Jonas qui aura 25 ans en l'an 2000.
   I. Tanner, Alain. II. Jonas qui aura 25 ans en l'an 2000 (Motion picture)
III. Title. IV. Title: Jonas qui aura 25 ans en l'an 2000. V. Title: Jonah
who will be twenty-five in the year 2000.
PN1997.J5613   1983   791.43'72   83-21992
ISBN 0-913028-97-5
ISBN 0-913028-98-3 (pbk.)

Contents:

Opening Credits

**Yves Gasser and Yves Peyrot
Present**

JONAH WHO WILL BE 25 IN THE YEAR 2000

With		
	Jean-Luc Bideau	as Max
	Myriam Boyer	as Mathilde
	Jacques Denis	as Marco
	Roger Jendly	as Marcel
	Dominique Labourier	as Marguerite
	Myriam Mezière	as Madeleine
	Miou-Miou	as Marie
	Rufus	as Mathieu

and with
Raymond Bussières

A Production of
**Citel Films Geneva
S.S.R.
Action Films Paris
S.F.P.**

A film by
Alain Tanner

Final Credits

Screenplay	John Berger and Alain Tanner
Adaptation and Dialogue	Alain Tanner
Director of Photography	Renato Berta
First Assistant	Carlo Varini
Second Assistant	Paule Muret
Production Manager	Bernard Lorain
Sound Engineer	Pierre Gamet
Assistant	Luc Yersin
Assistants to the Director	Laurent Ferrier Anita Peyrot Alain Klarer
Music	Jean-Marie Sénia
Editing	Brigitte Susselier Marc Blavet (Assistant)
Continuity	Anne-Marie Fallot
Set Designer	Yanko Hodjis Olivier Bierer (Assistant)
Still Photographer	Luc Chessex
Assistant Production Manager	Guy Michaud
Make-up	Michèle Pissanchi
Electricians	Robert Boner Benjamin Lehmann
Stage Hands	Jean-Pierre Goilard Robert Peyramaure
Production Supervisor	Roland Jouby
Executive Producer	Yves Peyrot
Deputy Producer	Yves Gasser

and with

Pierre Holdener
Maurice Anfair
Jean Schlegel
Gilbert Costa
Christine Wipf
Guillaume Chenevière
Robert Schmid
Daniel Stuffel
Francis Reusser
Michel Fidanza
Nicole Dié
Domingo Semedo
Mady Deluz
and the theater group of the Collège Calvin

Music Publication   Fanfan Musique

Laboratories   Cinégram   Geneva
                           G.T.C.   Paris

Censor's Certificate   45,442

Time, Place of Action, and Description of Characters

Place City and suburb of Geneva

Time About twenty-five years before the year 2000

The Characters

The eight principal characters will all be between fifty and sixty in the year 2000. Jonah, who is born two-thirds of the way through the story, will be twenty-five.

We have nicknamed our characters the "little prophets," first because their prophecies are little, and second because they themselves are not conscious of being prophets in the traditional sense of the term. They never announce their prophecies, which only exist for them at the individual and existential level (which does not mean that they lack generosity or are incapable of taking responsibility for their choices).

This is why they are also absurd, the way clowns can be. They would reply that it's the world around them which is absurd, and they would be right.

The century's great prophecies were political and revolutionary. The final moment of these prophecies in Western Europe and the United States was 1968. The prophecy has not been realized. The danger of the great prophecies is megalomania and the absence of scruples which sometimes accompanies them, and also sudden disillusionment.

Max

Max is disillusioned. Combatant during May '68, he believes that political history stopped on that date. He sees the future moving toward totalitarianism and fascism. This is not perversity on his part. In fact his vision of history is larger than that of the other characters. But he sees history as martyred. His hope had been revolutionary and this hope has become diminished, if not exhausted. This is probably why he would like to stop time. Max is a little bitter, but neither cynical nor defeated. The memory of '68 occasionally revives him. When that happens, he considers what is actually going on (self included) as trivial and without importance. He has an old man's attitude, or that of a father who believes that reality and grandeur belong to the past.

In this sense, alone among the eight, he is an ex-prophet.

Max is big, and like Brecht's elephant, he never forgets. In fact he would like to stop or suspend time. This is why he has become a devotee of gambling, in particular roulette. To earn a living he is a proofreader for a newspaper, and as soon as he has a little money he gambles. At the gaming table time no longer means anything. Everything is focussed on the result of the game—where the ball is going to stop. Nothing else has any importance. Everyone is alone before the wheel, as before death. The wheel which slows down and the impending result contain their own finality. But nothing is ever definitive: the wheel always begins to turn again. Every true gambler chooses to play with the goal of 1) becoming a loser in the world situated byeond the table and 2) living always in the same moment at the table, a moment from one's own past of which he is more or less conscious. For Max this moment is May '68, cherry-blossom time. Historically, the seven other little prophets are Max's offspring. They are survivors. Each of their little prophecies had its place in the great synthetic prophecy of 1968. In a sense Max is something like their father, even though he completely refuses his progeny. He is also a disappointed adolescent. In his character there is an unresolvable tragic element.

When he takes action regarding the real estate deal, it is both from a love of the game and to hold off his own self-disdain. This act will make him acceptable to the others.

Madeleine

Madeleine is a quick and efficient secretary employed by a temporary help agency. Her aim is to earn as much money as possible as quickly as possible. As soon as she has enough she leaves alone on a trip to distant countries. She is back from India and will return there, since her interest lies in tantrism. She tries with some success to apply its teachings, which are the fairest she knows of. She does it above all for herself, without trying to convert others.

Of the eight she is probably the most violent, since she is the most extreme and the most spontaneous, as well as the most absurd. She knows herself very well, but she is naive in believing she can transplant tantrism to Europe. She also tends a little to idealize Max, immediately taking him for a pure political militant.

She is self-assured and skilled at imposing her own rhythm (whether it be slow or fast).

15

Mathieu

Mathieu is a typographer by profession. he belongs—or rather used to belong—among the workers' elite. He was a union cadre. Unemployed for several months, he has changed, even though Lenin and Romain Rolland continue to reign over his library shelves.

He is married to Mathilde. They have three children, one adopted, and they are the parents of Jonah who will be born in the course of the story. Along the way he will first discover a certain liking for the work he finds at the truck-garden, then a true vocation for the educating of young children.

Mathieu is a character gifted with great natural authority, but he never makes undue use of it.

When his attempt at an alternative school fails, he will find himself once again forced to take whatever work comes along. He will go to work in a factory, with his "status" lowered relative to what it was previously, a situation he will know how to take advantage of by returning to the struggle on new terms.

Mathilde

Mathilde is Mathieu's wife and the mother of Jonah, her fourth child though she is only 28. During the time of her husband's unemployment and up until Jonah's birth, Mathilde works in an electrical equipment factory. She comes from a workers' environment, and she has the look of a child in a woman's body. It is her body, and those of others, which form her "familiar territory." With her body she maintains a full and friendly relationship. She very much likes being pregnant. Though it derives from no theory, she is an expert at massage. Despite the fatigue of her own overly full daily life, she is always ready to massage away the fatigue in the body of others.

Marcel

Marcel is a truck-gardener. He owns some land at the exit from the city and sells his vegetables at the market. Of all the characters, Marcel is the "craziest." That is, his alternative world is the most exclusive, the one depending least on contact with the "real" world. In another era he would have been a hermit. He is ascetic by

nature and has a passion for the animal world. He photographs the animals which live around him, without any artistic goal. Then from the photos he develops, he makes naive drawings which he keeps for himself. The photos cover the kitchen walls, but the drawings remain confined with him in the "secret room." Just as a true hunter—not a sportsman—depends physically upon animals, Marcel depends upon them spiritually. For him the world is a mystery, and animals offer certain explanations. In the so-called social order, he sees only disorder and the absence of mystery. He always speaks of his knowledge in this area. He is sententious but does not moralize. Even though he maintains very good relations with those in his entourage, humans for him are the least interesting animals.

Marguerite

She is Marcel's wife and the mother of two children between five and ten years old. As opposed to her husband, she thinks in sociopolitical terms. But her point of departure has nothing to do with "politics." She is interested in ecology, thus her emphasis on what relates to bio-agriculture. Her orientation: earth-excrement-rebirth. Of the eight she is the one most freely capable of discussing death. She always dresses in black, yet she if full of vitality. In the era when Marcel would have been a hermit, she would have been a sorceress. This possibly is the reason for their marriage. Marguerite's sense of the practical is highly developed. It is she who keeps the books, gives orders, sees to the selling. All the same she is more interested in astrology than political parties. She can discuss the moon while keeping the current market prices at the tips of her fingers.

She wishes for the overthrow of the capitalist system of industry and consumption.

Since Marcel is more interested in animals than in her, an odd state of affairs comes about: from time to time she has sexual relations with migrant workers living in the nearby barracks. To simplify the terms on both sides, she arranges to be paid a small amount for this.

To the children she is at once mother and father. Her rages are part of her generosity. She imposes on the children a practical but never moralistic discipline.

Marco

Marco is a high-school history instructor. History interests him, but not teaching. His methods of instruction are completely unorthodox and his knowledge of the official curriculum defective. For these reasons the students are very fond of him. Shuttled from one school to another he will quickly and definitively be barred from instruction, to which in any case he makes no effort whatsoever to adapt. At each new institution where he is sent before the final firing, Marco delivers an inaugural lesson which explores the mythology of instruction. Thanks to Marie, with whom he will fall in love, Marco will meet her aged friend Charles. And thanks to Charles he will discover that he is more skilled at engendering discussion with the old than with the young. Thus he will become an activities director in an old people's home where among other things his musical gifts will blossom.

Despite his apparent vivacity, Marco is perhaps the most private of the characters in the story.

Marie

Marie is a super-market check-out girl and a border-worker. Such "border-workers" live on the French side of the border while working in Switzerland.

They must return home every evening after work.

When Marie's fingers "miss" the keys on her cash register the price indicated will be inaccurate as will the price paid by her clients. In the store's daily accounting these errors — always undercharges of course — can only be attributed to theft. Thus Marie adds things up according to the customer's appearance, not systematically, but as the impulse seizes her. She is known to the pensioners who line up at her check-out stand. It's her way of telling people she loves them. One day it is Marco's turn to benefit from her generosity. But the trickery will end up being discovered. Arrested by the police and sent to prison for a period of six months, Marie is expelled from the country. Refusing any kind of alienated labor, she will return illegally to live with Marco on the other side of the border.

Marie is refusal, revolt, inarticulateness and risk. And also kindness.

Other Characters

Charles, former locomotive engineer for the French National Railroad, who lives near Annemasse, across the hall in Marie's apartment block. Widowed and slightly handicapped.

The two laborers who work for Marcel and Marguerite. Unwashed and uncouth, they are known as the primitives, or the two zeros.

The children: those of Mathilde and Mathieu, those of Marcel and Marguerite and a few others in the neighborhood.

The high-school students, around seventeen years old.

The old people in the retirement home.

The banker, de Vandoeuvres Jr., Bank of Geneva and Nassau.

A minor official at the same bank.

And Jonah, who will be born during the story, will be three months old at the end, five years old in the film's final shot.

The film is shot in color. Color is reality. When reality gives way to the imaginary, to the characters' dreams or their nightmares, the image changes to black and white, or eventually to an "altering" of the initial colors.

In order to simplify the text, scenes are shot in color where no indication is given and in black and white where so noted.

Quotations: J.J. Rousseau, Octavio Paz,
Samuel Butler, Pablo Neruda,
Adrian Mitchell, Jean Piaget

Scenario

Reel 1

Scene 1

1
long shot
interior
day

Tobacconist. Max enters, buys cigarettes.

MAX
Gauloises filters please.

SALESWOMAN *(she gives him the pack)*
One-ninety please.

MAX
One-ninety? Yesterday it was one-seventy.

SALESWOMAN
It's gone up. Everything goes up.

Max pays and leaves. Mathieu enters.

MATHIEU
A pack of Gauloises.

25

Caption: "The next morning"

Scene 2

2
Black & White
close shot
exterior
day
lateral track
right–left
voice off-camera
music over text
End of Black & White

Statue of J.J. Rousseau

"All our wisdom consists of servile preju-
dices; all our customs are nothing but en-
slavement, constraint and coercion. Civilized
man is born, lives and dies in slavery; at birth
he is sewn into swaddling clothes; at his
death he is nailed into a coffin. As long as he
retains human form, he is enchained by our
institutions . . . "

Scene 3

3
interior
day

*Apartment of Mathieu and Mathilde. They are
having breakfast with their children in the kitchen.
Mathilde is getting ready to go to work.*

MATHIEU
First thing this morning I'm going to see the
truck-gardeners.

MATHILDE
Where?

MATHIEU
The job. The little notice in the paper I read
you yesterday.

MATHILDE
Oh that. I have trouble imagining you surrounded by salad

MATHIEU
Why? I have trouble imagining you surrounded by machines and little bosses. In the
serenity of work. They're devouring you
Mathilde. They're devouring my wife. As a

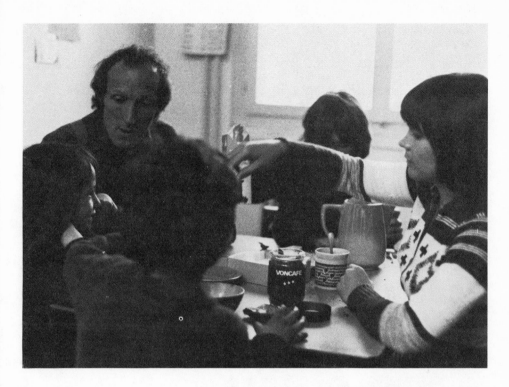

result I'm sure we're turning into the organs of our enemies, their guts and balls. And when they've had their fill they'll toss you into the street, like they did with me.

MATHILDE
Don't forget to dress the children warmly when they leave for school. And make something besides noodles for dinner. There's been enough of that. Everyone's a little fed up. Find a vegetable.

MATHIEU
O.K. my love. A vegetable.

Scene 4

4
close shot
interior
day

Mathilde is in the bus which takes her to work. The bus crosses the Mont-Blanc bridge. It passes the Ile Rousseau. The statue of Rousseau is visible on its pedestal.

27

Scene 5

5 long shot interior day	*Electrical equipment factory. Mathilde is at work among the other laborers. Her work is simple, repetitive and without interest*
6 close shot interior day *Black & White*	*Mathilde working at a press. A foreman with a pocketwatch in his hand passes behind her.*
7 close up interior day	*Mathilde's hands massaging the foreman's back.*
8 interior day	*The foreman is sleeping on his stomach on a table, naked to the waist. Mathilde vigorously massages his back, the nape of his neck and his shoulders.*

FOREMAN
At school I lost every race.

Usually stiff and nervous, the foreman is now as submissive and relaxed as a child.

End of Black & White

Scene 6

9 and 10 long shot exterior day	*Region of Marcel and Marguerite Certoux's house. Fields and truck-gardens. Marguerite is working in one of them on a tractor.*
	Mathieu is on a motor bike. He arrives near Marcel's house. He stops, having noticed a woman working in a garden. It is Marguerite.
11 close shot exterior day	MATHIEU Hello, I'm looking for Marcel Certoux's house. Do you know it?

MARGUERITE
Yes. I'm Marguerite Certoux. You're here about the job?

MATHIEU
Yes. I saw the little notice in the paper and I'm interested.

MARGUERITE
You've done this kind of work?

MATHIEU
No, but I can learn. Is it difficult?

MARGUERITE
No. That is, yes. You have to love it.

12
close shot

MARGUERITE
What kind of work do you do?

MATHIEU
I'm an manual laborer.

MARGUERITE
A manipulator?

MATHIEU
No, manual labor. Or work if you prefer. I'm
labor. So I'm for hire. I've been unemployed
for three months. I have two children plus a
third, adopted.

MARGUERITE
If you're labor, what do you make of me?

MATHIEU
You don't exactly resemble capital.

13
close shot
exterior
day
forward track
follows them from
behind

Mathieu and Marguerite walking

*Black & White
continuation of same
scene*

MATHIEU
You'll show me the books. I insist that as part
of my wages.

MARGUERITE
If you like.

MATHIEU
You agree?

MARGUERITE
I've nothing to hide. But why do you want to
look at them?

MATHIEU
Simply to find out whether the going rate is
fair. Usually that isn't done. It's never done.

End of Black & White

31

Scene 7

14
close up
interior
day
Pan from below up,
from the chicken
to Marcel's face
then to Mathieu's

*Marcel's house. Marguerite and Mathieu are in
kitchen. Marcel is plucking a chicken.*

MATHIEU
Then I'm hired?

MARGUERITE
I think so. You're hired.

lateral track
left close to
Marguerite's face

MATHIEU
What will I have to do?

MARGUERITE
You get up early. On market days you'll load
the pick-up. You'll also have to bring in the
manure. The others don't much want to
anymore.

MATHIEU
How many are there?

reverse track
framing
Mathieu and
Marguerite
in close
medium shot

MARGUERITE
You and the two zeros, zero-one and
zero-two.

MARCEL
The two idiots.

MATHIEU
They're idiots?

MARGUERITE
No, but a bit primitive.

MATHIEU
And the manure's from the peasants?

continuous
lateral
traverse
right to left
framing Marguerite
in profile

MARGUERITE
No, the horses. Horseshit to make vegetables grow. No chemical fertilizers for us.
But it's difficult, the profits are obviously
smaller, the work harder.

MATHIEU
And horseshit is best?

continuous
lateral track
passes behind
Marguerite and
frames Mathieu
and Marcel

MARGUERITE
No, but the peasants keep the cowshit for
themselves, and since there are plenty of
riding schools . . . All those useless horses
turning in a circle do at least one intelligent
thing.

MARCEL
They shit.

MARGUERITE
How did you lose your job?

continuous
lateral track,
frames
Mathieu's
profile in
close up

MATHIEU
Crisis at the printer. Reduction of
personnel.

MARGUERITE
You were a typographer?

MATHIEU
Yes.

MARGUERITE
And since you were a union militant you
were the first to go.

MARCEL
Here with the two zeroes you won't have
much chance for labor agitating. You could
form a union of zeroes. You'd be zero-
three.

MATHIEU
I'd rather be called by my name. Mathieu.
Mathieu Vernier. When do I begin?

MARGUERITE
Tomorrow if you'd like.

*Mathieu looks at the walls which are covered with
photographs of animals.*

lateral track
right–left
behind Marguerite,
reframing Marcel
and receding to
opposite long
shot

MATHIEU
You're the one who took these photos?

MARCEL
I'm the one.

MATHIEU
You don't photograph people?

music over
the receding
shot

MARCEL
Never.

34

MARGUERITE
Not even his own children. Only little animals. Afterwards he sketches them.

end of music

MATHIEU
Really?

MARCEL
They're more interesting than us. Or if you
like, we are the less interesting animals.
With us it's chaos. Not them. And with
people there's no mystery.

MARGUERITE
He only likes the two zeros. Same with me.
A little.

MARCEL
That's because you're a sorceress. And the
zeros resemble animals. Do you like animals?

MATHIEU
Sure, more or less.

Scene 8

15
long shot
exterior
day

*Balcony of the farm. Mathieu is getting ready to
leave but Marcel detains him.*

MARCEL
Did you know that whales are among the few
animals whose voices are not expressive?

MATHIEU
Meaning?

MARCEL
O.K., when a dog barks or a cat meows they
express themselves that way. And they can
express themselves in lots of different ways.
Whales simply emit coded sounds (he imi-
tates), but without varying the expression.

35

Maybe someday mathematics will help us understand them. And do you know what some sailors discovered in the open sea of the Kamtchatka? Huge grey-pink islands, unknown, not marked on the charts. And do you know what they were?

MATHIEU
No.

MARCEL
Huge piles of shrimp, shrimp conglomerates. And do you know why there are islands of shrimp and why we'll be swallowing shrimp for breakfast, in our soup, for dessert and with our coffee?

MATHIEU
No, I don't know.

MARCEL
O.K., it's because we've killed all the whales to make lipstick and since whales eat shrimp and since they can't any more because we've murdered them, we're all going to croak from shrimp indigestion. That'll be it for our fat faces.

MATHIEU (takes Marcel's hand)
See you tomorrow.

a few notes of music
over the end

Scene 9

16
long shot
interior
day

Class at Geneva High School. The students, boys and girls, are about sixteen or seventeen years old. The principal of the high school introduces Marco, the new history teacher.

THE PRINCIPAL
I would like to introduce your new history teacher, Mr. Marco Perly, who beginning today is replacing Mr. Genthod who, as you know, has just retired. Please give him a nice welcome.

The principal leaves. Marco, who has been holding a suitcase, puts it down on the desk and opens it. He takes out a long piece of sausage, a small block, a cleaver and a metronome, all of which he shows to the amused and surprised students.

MARCO
Never forget that my father is a butcher and that my mother sings light opera very well.

Laughter. He lays the sausage on the cutting block and flourishes the cleaver, then sets the metronome going.

MARCO
Would someone like to come and cut the sausage? In time with the metronome . . .

37

A boy rushes forward and begins to cut the sausage. Screams and laughter from the class.

MARCO
Good, that's enough for now.

The boy stops. Marco picks up a few pieces of the cut sausage.

forward
tracking shot
until Marco
is framed in
close shot

MARCO
So these are the pieces of history. What should we call them? Hours? Decades? Centuries? It's all the same and it never stops. The sausage is eaten with mashed potatoes. Is time a sausage? Darwin thought so, even though the stuffing changed from one end of the sausage to the other. Marx thought that some day everyone would stop eating sausage. Einstein and Max Planck tore the skin off the sausage which from then on lost its shape. What is sausage skin made of?

A GIRL
Pig's intestine.

MARCO
Very good. Now let's look at the sausage that hasn't been cut up yet. You can see creases, folds. And that's what I want to talk to you about. What are time's folds made of?

17
very close shot
interior
day
track right–left
across faces of
students listening

Music over start
of tracking shot
and entire text

In agricultural societies, men believed that time consisted simply of cycles, of seasons. Each winter solstice contained the same moment. An individual grew old of course, but that was simply because he wore himself out: he was the fuel which made the machine of the seasons go. Capitalism will supply the idea of time-as-highway. Highway of the sun, the highway of progress. The idea of progress was that the conquerers hadn't simply won a battle, but that they had been chosen and designated because they were superior beings. Their superiority would

inevitably span the cycles and the seasons. It transformed them into cork-screws of which they, the conquerers, were the tip. And with that tip they opened the bottles of the lesser cultures, one after another. They drank until their thirst was quenched and tossed aside the bottles, assuring themselves that they would break. This was a new kind of violence. The arrow or the sword had previously killed, but what killed now was the verdict of history. The history of the conquerers of course. With this new violence arose a new fear among the conquerers: the fear of the past, fear of the lesser beings in their broken bottles.

end of music

18
close shot of
Marco
interior
day

Ah! if only the past could one day overtake the conquerers, it would certainly show as little pity as they themselves had shown. During the nineteenth century, this fear of the past was transformed rationally into scientific law. Time then became a road without curves. The length of the road was a terrifying abstraction, but abstractions don't take revenge. From that point on the thinkers of the nineteenth century opted for the fear of thought while eliminating the fear of the savage and his arrows. And their roads had boundaries. Absolutely regular. Millions of years divided into eras, into dates, into days and into hours of work to punch in on the time-clock. Like sausage.

Scene 10

19
long shot
interior
day
pan left–right
following Max

Max's apartment. Morning. Max gets up, sits on the edge of his bed and leafs through the newspaper as he's waking. There are newspapers everywhere. He puts down his paper and goes over to a bureau to take out a piece of clothing. He opens a drawer.

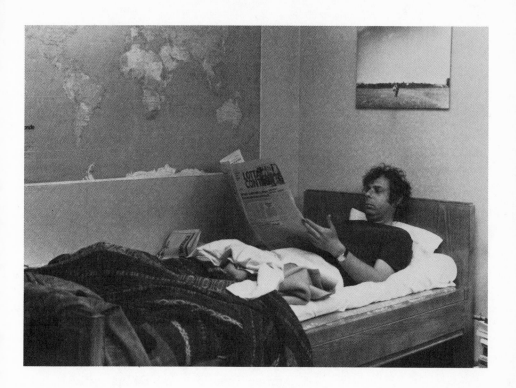

20
Black & White
close up
drawer & revolver
pan left-right
following Max
frame in close
medium shot

End of Black & White

Inside the drawer is a revolver. Max takes it and aims at his reflection in the mirror. On the bureau is an alarm clock. Max aims at it and fires. The clock flies to pieces.

Scene 11

21
close shot of
Marco
interior
day
reverse tracking shot
preceding Marco

MARCO
In short we see today that the highway, the highway of capitalism, is collapsing. For more reasons than I can recount to you in the little fragment of sausage which this inaugural lecture is. In an acorn are already present the creases which will give the oak its

41

who walks toward
his desk. Class at
the school.
Marco's inagural
lecture.

shape. What you are, each one of you, was already present in the chromosomes at the moment of my conception. Excuse me, your conception. I'm not a determinist, but in your first cell there was a message which you are now in the process of reading. There are things which make holes in time.

He goes to the blackboard and makes a drawing.

forward tracking
shot toward
Marco who is
seated at
his desk

MARCO
And the holes line up perfectly (he draws). You can run a spit right through. Don't forget that my father is a butcher. Time bends so that the holes can coincide. And why is one never a prophet in his own land? Because prophets only get halfway through the holes, like this. (he pantomimes)

Music

They exist between times. No one understood much about Diderot until an entire generation screamed "Monster" at Freud. That much time was needed to pass through the hole. The holes prophets make for look-

Reverse track
in center to
long shot
of class

ing into the future are the same through which historians later peer at the stuff of the past. Look at them leering through the holes dug by Jean-Jacques Rousseau in order to explain the eighteenth century to us.

End of music

You're looking at your watches. O.K. Time's up. We'll finish with a binary rhythm, the rhythm of the heart and of drummers.

He begins to beat rhythmically on his desk.

MARCO
Between each beat there is time. Time is the fact of recognizing that the second beat is not the first. Time is created by opposition.

He beats on the desk and some of the students take up his lead. Laughter and screams throughout the class.

MARCO
Through synthesis time grows smaller.

The rhythm of the drumming intensifies. The whole class bangs on their desks. Marco is forced to yell.

MARCO
The human embryo whistles across the entire span of evolution!

He whistles with his fingers. Some students imitate him.
The drumming continues growing faster and louder, the class goes wild. Screams and laughter. Marco howls.

MARCO
With total synthesis, time disappears.

The bell rings, signalling the end of class.

End of Reel 1

Reel 2

Scene 12

22
close up
interior
day

Mathilde opening the door.
Apartment of Mathieu and Mathilde. Kitchen.
Mathieu is preparing dinner. Mathilde returns
from work.

MATHILDE
I'm falling apart, my love. Into little pieces.

23
very close shot

reverse tracking shot
to medium shot of
Mathilde in
the field

Mathieu sitting at the table

MATHIEU
Don't do that to yourself—it's going to work
out. There are other things. First of all, I've
found a job.

MATHILDE
With the truck-gardeners?

MATHIEU
Yes.

MATHILDE
It's O.K.?

MATHIEU
It seems to be. Fresh air, vegetables, selling at
the market.

MATHILDE
You, selling at the market?

MATHIEU
Sure, I'll do fine.

MATHILDE
And the owners?

MATHIEU
Pleasant. The guy's a little strange. He tells
stories about murdered whales and huge
piles of shrimp. But there's even more. I've
found an apartment too.

MATHILDE
An apartment?

MATHIEU
It comes with the job.

Lateral track
left to right to   MATHILDE
framing of Mathilde   Incredible. Is it big?
in foreground
with Mathieu   MATHIEU
coming and standing   Very big. Old. In a country house. With
behind her   fields, gardens and birds. It's the wheel of
                                       fortune turning, as the idiots on the radio
                                       would say.

MATHILDE
We won't knock it.

MATHIEU
Definitely not.

MATHILDE
How big is it?

MATHIEU
Big—big. A huge pile of rooms.

Music

MATHILDE
There won't be enough of us to live there.
I think it's time you gave me a child. I don't
like empty spaces. Or my empty belly. Or my
empty breasts. I want to be invaded, to over-
flow. Mathieu, in nine months I'll be as big as

End of music

this (*she demonstrates*).

Scene 13

24
interior at night
medium tracking
shot right to left
across the
roulette table

*X's casino. Roulette room and table. A few players,
Max among them in the midst of playing roulette.
What is important here is not the atmosphere or the
appearance of the players but the essence of the
game, that is the wheel itself and the ball.*

Tango music

MAX
The thirty-two.

THE CROUPIER
Place your bets. No more bets.

Scene 14

25
interior at night
medium shot
Max at the bar

*Bar of the casino, a little later. Max is drinking a
coffee. The banker de Vandoeuvres with his secretary Madeleine sit down close to Max. De Van-
oeuvres is obviously drunk.*

DE VANDOEUVRES
Satigny! Don't you recognize me? (to
Madeleine) We were in school together.

MAX
Yes, I recognize you.

DE VANDOEUVRES
What are you doing here?

Max, irritated by this encounter, doesn't answer.

DE VANDOEUVRES
You're drinking coffee . . . Come on, I'll buy you whiskey.

MAX
No thanks, this is fine.

DE VANDOEUVRES
Come on! Even revolutionaries drink whiskey these days . . . Tell me, did you go to the wrong church this evening? Are you playing to refill the party's coffers? What were you before? Commie-bolshi-what? Come on, I'm buying. I've lost a pile tonight.

MAX
Come on, you're not entirely ruined yet. What are you selling these days?

DE VANDOEUVRES
I'm selling wind. The wind rises, flows, passes over a hard-working humanity and me, I stand at the end with a scoop to pick up the pennies.

He then tries to stand up straight, as if to introduce himself.

DE VANDOEUVRES
De Vandoeuvres, Director, Bank of Geneva and Nassau, a Christmas gift from daddy.

He turns toward Madeleine. She has been very attentive to Max whom she glances at with a look of complicity.

DE VANDOEVRES
This is Madeleine, quick, efficient secretary, as well as temporary.

MAX *(to Madeleine)*
Pleased to meet you.

MADELEINE
Good evening.

MAX *(to Vandoeuvres)*
Nassau, that's in the Bermudas or the
Bahamas?

DE VANDOEUVRES
The Bahamas.

MAX
You have business there?

DE VANDOEUVRES
No, vacations. I do business here. Right now
I'm going to do some amazing business here.

*He takes a few glasses and tries to depict the scene,
but with difficulty due to his drunkenness.*

26
close up
interior
night
tracking shot left to
right and back
Max in profile at left
De V. from behind at
the center and
Madeleine in profile
at right winking in
complicity at Max

DE VANDOEUVRES
Here, between the suburbs and the country.
Right here, where rezoning occurs at the
right moment. We have to empty the center
of the cities. There are too many people.
Also people love the country. We're going
to build deluxe suburban shacks there.

Scene 15

27
Exterior
day
close up, forward
tracking shot from

49

behind of Madeleine
who is walking in the
street

28
exterior
day
close up, reverse
tracking shot from
in front of
Madeleine walking

A musical chord

Black & White

29
long shot of tantric
erotic painting

End of Black & White

Scene 16

30
interior
day
close up of the
offices of the Bank
of Geneva and
Nassau

A musical chord

Black & White

31
medium shot
lateral tracking to
the left of the office
manager who leaves
his place and comes
toward Madeleine
lying naked on her
desk. He has a nap-
kin around his neck,
sits down and with
his fingers eats the
food on Madeleine's
belly.

End of Black & White

32
long shot
forward track and
pan right to left
following Madeleine
who goes toward
Max at the door

Madeleine is typing. She stops and gazes at the office manager, as if in a dream.

Bank of Geneva and Nassau. Max is brought into a room where Madeleine is working. She recognizes him and comes to him.

MADELEINE
Hello. What are you doing here? Do you want to see De Vandoeuvres?

MAX
No, you. It's you I want to see.

MADELEINE
Oh? That's nice. I'm glad.

MAX *(he is a little disturbed and talks in a low voice)* Do you have a moment? Time for a coffee. I have something to ask you.

MADELEINE
If you like. It sounds important.

MAX
It is important. But I can't talk about it here. Can you leave?

MADELEINE
Yes, in five minutes. I'm finishing a letter.

MAX
I'll wait for you downstairs, in the cafe at the corner.

MADELEINE
O.K.

She looks at Max as if he were about to announce he was in love with her.

Scene 17

33
very close shot
with lateral tracking
left—right—left,
passing from one to
to the other
interior
day

A few minutes later. Max and Madeleine are having coffee in the cafe at the corner.

MAX
All the same be careful not to get caught.

MADELEINE
I'll make the copies after everyone's gone.

MAX
Is all the information in the file?

MADELEINE
I think so. The names of all the owners involved are, in any case.

MAX
I bet it's the classic speculative move involving zoning changes. Vandoeuvres has political friends, he has great sources.

MADELEINE
In exchange they are going to offer them plots further out, in the country, and with the threat of expropriation.

MAX
And three years later they'll turn the whole thing over at four times the price.

MADELEINE
Are you going to talk to the people in the district? Spill the whole thing?

MAX
No, I don't think so. I'm only going to warn them about the move being prepared, but without revealing details. If they don't sell, we'll see the price go up and up . . . and it will be for them to draw conclusions, not me.

34
long shot
interior
day
same place
musical chord at
the cut

MADELEINE
What do you do in life?

MAX *(evasively)*
Nothing special. I work for a newspaper.

MADELEINE
Are you going to write articles about your
tours of the district?

MAX
No. I don't write anymore. I'm a proofreader. I correct the fuck-ups of others.
That leaves my mind free. And you, besides
typing the fuck-ups of others, what do you
do?

MADELEINE
I earn as much money as possible as quickly
as possible and then I take off.

MAX
Where to?

MADELEINE
Far away. Last time to India, and I'm going
back.

MAX
Alone?

MADELEINE
Yes.

MAX
I'll bet you run charter tours for rich hippies.
Or else you're looking for God.

MADELEINE
Already found him.

35
very close shot
interior

MAX
What's he like?

day
same place
lateral track with
inverse pan going
from one to the
other
musical chord
at the cut

Madeleine puts her index finger on Max's forehead.

MADELEINE
He's here. (*She recites, amused*) He is in the silent explosion which opens the lotus at the top of your skull when you make love standing up, so that you hold in the seed and let it rise, transcendent, the length of your spine to here.

Once again she places her index finger on Max's forehead.

MADELEINE
It's the conjunction of all the energies which come to make the great void, the thought that has no object.

MAX
Oh my! In vulgar parlance we call that a fuck
which splits your gourd open.

MADELEINE
Very vulgar, yes. But it isn't a matter of that.
I'll show you some day, if you like. If you can.

MAX
Usually I prefer otherwise, but why not. The
thought without object, that must be like
what one feels playing roulette. The photo-
copies, when can you make them for me?

MADELEINE
This evening.

MAX
Quick and efficient, as Vandoeuvres says.
Your lotus thing, is it Zen or Tantra?

MADELEINE
Tantra.

musical chord at the
end

Scene 18

36
long shot
exterior
day

*Balcony of Marcel's house. Marco, who lives next
door, knocks at the entrance and Marguerite opens
the door.*

MARCO
Good evening.

MARGUERITE
Good evening. How are you?

MARCO
Fine. I wanted to see if you had any cabbages.

MARGUERITE
Yes. But right now I've got a soup cooking.
Ask Mathieu, the new one who lives downstairs, he'll get it for you. Is it for your
supper?

MARCO
No, it's for my history lesson.

MARGUERITE
Oh? Are you having supper alone?

MARCO
Yes.

MARGUERITE
Come eat with us in a few minutes.

MARCO
O.K. Thank you.

MARGUERITE
We'll expect you.

Scene 19

37
medium shot
exterior
day

Marco and Mathieu are in a garden near the house. Mathieu has picked a cabbage.

MARCO
Have you ever noticed that when you cut a cabbage in half the designs made by the leaves resemble the convolutions of the brain?

MATHIEU
Are you a botany or anatomy teacher?

MARCO
History. I'll also need some seeds so that we

can plant them and watch them come up.
Right now we are studying the question of
time. Time passing.

MATHIEU
Oh, right.

38
long shot
exterior
day
reverse tracking shot
preceding Mathieu
and Marco who are
heading toward the
farm
finish in medium

MARCO
What does a cabbage cost these days?

MATHIEU
It's by weight. About two-ninety a kilo.

MARCO
Expensive. That one weighs at least two
kilos.

MATHIEU
It's inflation.

MARCO
Everyone says that. Beer for two francs in a
cafe, it's inflation. Cabbages, that's inflation.
And no one knows what it's about. There are
buzz words like that, with no meaning left.
More and more of them. Inflation . . .

MATHIEU
Me, I know what inflation is.

MARCO
Really? Could you explain this phenomenon
clearly?

MATHIEU
Of course. Why?

MARCO
Because the other day my students asked me
the exact meaning of the word, and the
workings of the thing, and I couldn't explain
it to them. They were angry. They were right
to be.

MATHIEU
Well sure, a history teacher.

MARCO *(amazed)*
"Well sure." And you, you'd know how to explain it to them?

MATHIEU
Yes.

A few notes of music
repeated three or
four times

MARCO
Would you like to come to my class one day
and give a lesson in inflation? I do that from
time to time. I invite people to speak.

MATHIEU
Sure, I agree. On two conditions.

MARCO
Which are?

MATHIEU
First that I have enough time and second
that I may tell the truth.

MARCO
You will have the whole hour. As for the
truth, that goes without saying.

MATHIEU
Ah no. That doesn't go without saying.

MARCO
Then I'm telling you.

MATHIEU
You take risks. The truth in school . . .

MARCO *(amused)*
It's not the first time.

39
day
interior
forward track

*Marcel is drawing a dog. He is surrounded by
stuffed animals and drawings.*

toward Marcel in his
"secret room"

Scene 20

40
medium shot
interior
night

*Evening meal in Marcel's kitchen. Marco is at
table with the two zeros. They are waiting for the
owners, Marcel and Marguerite.*

ZERO ONE
Why are we waiting to eat?

ZERO TWO
We're waiting for Marcel.

ZERO ONE
We're always waiting for him. Where is he?

ZERO TWO
In his darkroom, I bet. Or in his secret room.

MARCO
Always photography, the boss?

ZERO TWO
He photographs chickens and then later he
sketches them.

He taps his temple with his index finger.

ZERO TWO
It's there, in the head.

ZERO ONE
It's not chickens. It's buzzards. Me, I'm
hungry.

MARCO
And Marguerite?

ZERO TWO
She'll be back. *(shrewd smile)* She went over to
the barracks.

MARCO
To the barracks?

ZERO ONE
Of the Italians.

ZERO TWO
It's Spaniards.

ZERO ONE
There are Italians too. And some Yugo-
slavians and some Greeks. Even Turks it
seems.

ZERO TWO
Turks—that should work out!

MARCO
She sells them vegetables?

Laughter.

ZERO TWO
Not vegetables, no. Something else.

They exchange amused looks.

MARCO
What then?

ZERO ONE
It only costs them twenty francs, it seems, for
a tumble.

ZERO TWO
It's not expensive. Marguerite enjoys it.
Marcel not so much.

ZERO ONE
Stop. We'll get into trouble.

MARCO
You've got some imagination.

reverse track to
re-frame in close-up

Marcel enters the kitchen.

MARCEL
Marguerite's not here?

ZERO ONE
She went out for a walk. Toward the barracks, I think.

Marcel immediately changes the subject.

MARCEL *(to Marco)* You're eating with us?
(to the Zeros) The soup's ready, right there on
the stove. What are you waiting for?

ZERO TWO
You. We're always waiting for you. With
your schemes . . .

MARCEL
You don't have much patience. *(to Marco)* Do
you know what a tick is?

MARCO
Yes. A tiny insect which sucks the blood of
animals.

MARCEL
Exactly. I'll serve the soup and then I'll tell
you something about the tick.

Scene 21

41
long shot
exterior
night

*Marguerite arrives at the door of a barrack near
her house, accompanied by a man. The man leaves
her and enters the barrack. Marguerite departs in
the direction of her house.*

Black & White

42-44
A few still photos

showing migrant
workers in their
barracks
musical chord
(percussion)

End of Black & White

Scene 22

45
close shot
interior
night
lateral track shot
left to right and pan
right to left until it
frames the entire
kitchen as
Marguerite enters

Marcel's kitchen, sequel to Scene 21

MARCEL
A tick lives for one day. It falls from the leaf
of a tree onto a warm-blooded animal, it
swallows the blood, it falls to the ground
when it's stuffed, it lays its eggs and it croaks.
The eggs hatch the tick which comes out,
climbs back up a tree and waits on a leaf for a
warm-blooded animal to pass.

Start of music over
tracking shot

ZERO TWO *(to Zero One)*
You for example. An animal who stinks.

MARCO
It distinguishes by scent? And if no animal
passes under its leaf it flies off?

MARCEL
No. It can only let itself fall. So it waits. And
you know how long it can wait *(to the Zeros)*
without eating?

End of music

MARCO
No.

MARCEL
It can wait eighteen years.

MARCO
Eighteen years? That's not true.

MARCEL
Yes, it's true. It's incredible. Eighteen years.

ZERO ONE
Eighteen years my ass. Without eating?

MARCEL
Without eating, idiot. And you two baboons can't wait five minutes.

Marguerite enters the kitchen.

ZERO TWO
Eighteen years.

MARGUERITE
Good evening. You've started? I'm a little late.

MARCO
Good evening.

He returns to his thoughts.

MARCO
The same creature that lives its entire life in
one day can wait eighteen years for that day.
Two completely different time scales in the
same tiny insect . . .

MARGUERITE
What? The tick . . . Marcel will bore your ass
off with his stories. Have you finished,
children? Off to bed!

The children leave.

ZERO ONE AND ZERO TWO *(to the
children)*
Good night.

46
close shot
interior

MARCEL
And where has the sorceress been?

night
on the other axis
framing Marcel and
Marguerite, then
lateral track right
to left toward Max's
arrival in close up
then reverse track to
close up of kitchen

MARGUERITE
For a walk. You know. I don't want to talk
about it.

MARCEL
It's nature's great mystery. In nature everything is mystery.

MARGUERITE
People are acting strange, there must be a
full moon tonight.

A knock at the door.

MARCEL
Come in.

It's Max. He stops at doorstep..

MAX
Good evening. I'm sorry, I'm disturbing you.
You're having dinner. I'll introduce myself:
Max Satigny. Is Mr. Certoux here?

MARCEL
That's me.

MAX
I have to talk to you about something important, but I can come back if I'm disturbing
you.

MARCEL
No, you're not disturbing us. Come in and sit
down. Marguerite, bring a glass.

MARGUERITE
You say it's something important?

ZERO ONE
It's because of the full moon.

MAX
No, it's something else. *(to Marcel)* Maybe it

would be better if I saw you alone for a
moment. It's a matter of real estate.

MARGUERITE
Real estate?

MARCEL *(indicating the others)*
That's my wife. These are the workers. This
is a neighbor, Mr. Perly. You can speak
freely here.

ZERO TWO
You're big.

MAX
Oh absolutely! Since I was small. Big like an
elephant. I also have a memory like an elephant. O.K. In a few words, this is what
it's about. They're in the process of putting
together a pretty big speculative venture tar-
getting the land in the district. Yours is included. The goal is obviously to screw
people. I'm here to warn you. I'm going
around the district.

MARGUERITE
What kind of venture?

MAX
You'll see. For now I advise you simply to refuse any purchase offer that may be made,
and see what follows.

MARCO
But how do you know about this? And who's
going to try to pull it off?

MAX
It's some company or other. And a friend of
mine told me about it who works in a bank
that's going to finance the deal.

MARCEL
Are you sure about this? You don't work for
the competition?

MAX
No, I swear. I've seen the whole file. You will
receive a letter and then a guy will come to
see you.

MARGUERITE
Thanks for warning us. But why are you
doing it?

MAX
Just for that. To see what will happen. It
interests me. I'll come back to see you.

He drinks.

MAX
Your health.

ZERO TWO
It's because you like vegetables.

MAX
Of course, that too. Braised lettuce stuffed
with bacon.

MARGUERITE
You're in politics.

MAX
Politics isn't worth it anymore.

Scene 23

47 & 48
Black & White

*Pictures from newsreels suggesting the eternal
game of the great powers.*

A few notes of music
(percussion)

Swiss army military parade.

49

*Salute from the presidium of the Supreme
Soviet.*

50   *Soviet rocket in Red Square during a*
                             military parade.

End of Black & White

End of Reel 2

Reel 3

Scene 24

51
medium shot
interior
day
reverse track then
forward following
Marco

*Supermarket. Marco has done his shopping and is
pushing his cart toward the check-out stands.
There are few people. Most of the check-out stands
are empty except for one, Marie's, where four or
five old people are in line. Curious and attracted
by Marie, Marco gets into her line. The time comes
for him to pay.*

52
close shot

Marco at Marie's check-out stand.

MARIE
That's ten francs forty.

MARCO
You're mistaken. You only counted the soil
(he has three sacks of soil in his cart) and you
forgot the whiskey (which was in fact
perfectly visible).

MARIE
No. I never make mistakes.

MARCO
But I assure you the whiskey alone is worth
forty francs.

MARIE
Ten francs forty please. You don't want to
tell me how to do my job, do you?

She throws a quick glance at Marco.

MARCO
Oh . . . well O.K., here it is.

He pays ten francs forty

53
close up of Marie

MARIE
Don't forget your change.

Scene 25

54
long shot
exterior
day

Marie is hitchhiking on a suburban road. A large Mercedes stops. Marie gets into the back seat.

55
close up
interior
day

The driver is surprised.

DRIVER
You wouldn't prefer to sit in the front?

56 close shot of Marie	MARIE No, I'd rather stay in the back.

Black & White

57 close shot of Marie singing (accompanied by piano and drums)	MARIE "If you never spend your money you know you'll always have some cash. If you stay cool and never burn you'll never turn to ash. If you lick the boots that kick you then you'll never feel the lash, and if you crawl along the ground at least you'll never crash. So why why why— WHAT MADE YOU THINK YOU COULD FLY?"

End of Black & White

Scene 26

58 long shot interior day pan left to right	*Printing shop where Max works. Madeline enters* *and is taken to Max's office.* MAX Well! What a surprise! The lotus flower!

59 medium shot interior day Max's office	MAX It's coming along. I've seen a lot of people. MADELEINE They'll begin making offers soon. They'll be gnashing their teeth. It's going to be amusing. *Interlude. Madeleine observes the surroundings.* MADELEINE There's one thing I still don't understand.

MAX
What?

MADELEINE
You.

MAX
Me?

MADELEINE
Yes. This ridiculous job. The roulette and
then your activity in this real estate affair.
It's difficult to put it all together.

MAX
No. Why? Well, maybe it is.

MADELEINE
Do you belong to some group?

MAX
No more. Before, yes.

MADELEINE
Before what?

MAX
In the sixties: '64, '65, '66, '67, '68
he traces a rising curve

'69, '70, '71, '72
he traces a descending curve

MADELEINE
May, '68 disgusted you?

MAX
No. Of course not. It's what followed.

MADELEINE
O.K. And I'm taking you out of this horrible
office. We're spending the evening together.
And the night.

MAX *(surprised)*
We're going for a drink?

MADELEINE
No, I'm taking you for carousel rides. To
the fair.

MAX
Oh, good idea.

Scene 27

60
medium shot
exterior
day
lateral track
left to right

Max and Madeleine are walking along the Rhone.

MADELEINE
And the roulette?

MAX
Oh that! That's death, time stopping,
chance, God the Father in a little ball, the
only place where he keeps total control, with
his big white beard.

MADELEINE
So you win?

MAX
No, I lose. Everyone goes to the casino to
lose. They don't know it but that's their
deepest motivation, the desire to be a loser.
The casinos, they know it. True happiness is
losing everything.

61
close shot
exterior
day

*Max and Madeleine from the back leaning against
the railing beside the Rhone.*

MADELEINE
Normally this kind of disillusionment comes
later. Around forty-five, when one begins to
see from the other side, and hopes have gone
unrealized. One would always like history to
advance at the speed of a man's life, and that
doesn't happen. As for me, I thought that

75

you were an activist because of this real estate
business.

MAX
Well no, you see. No longer.

Scene 28

62
medium shot
interior
day

*Charles's apartment, near Annemasse. Marie
enters the kitchen with the basket of provisions.*

CHARLES
Did you find everything?

MARIE
Found everything, Charles.

CHARLES
Pay for everything?

MARIE
What you find belongs to you. Others
have only to stop leaving things around.
I find things.

CHARLES
Marie, this is going to end badly. This
upsets me.

MARIE
It musn't Charles. Tell yourself that it's
part of the pension the railroad is
offering you. You've spent your whole
life driving locomotives.

CHARLES
But I enjoyed it.

MARIE
Then it's perfect. Are you feeling all
right?

CHARLES
Yes, fine, but I'm a little bored. You're
the first person I've seen today.

MARIE
You didn't go out?

CHARLES
No, I was waiting for you.

They are sitting at the kitchen table.

MARIE
Would you like to take a trip?

CHARLES
No, I'm thinking of a port of call. Full of
adventure.

MARIE
Where?

CHARLES
At Béziers, in 1935. In July. There was a
heatwave. I was almost killed. Across
from the station there was a bistro called
the Travellers Cafe, and the bistro had a
magnificent proprietress.

MARIE
And her husband was jealous.

CHARLES
Like a tiger. You guessed it.

MARIE
Should I play the proprietress?

CHARLES
No. She didn't resemble you at all. She was a
very imposing figure, the way the fashion
was then. Today, with your little behinds in
your little slacks . . . The railwaymen knew
her well. Her husband was an old cuckold.
She had taken him on with the business—it
always happens that way. This was my
chance, I spent every other night in Béziers.

77

She was named Rose, appropriately. What are you thinking about?

MARIE
I'm trying to imagine you, you and Rose.

CHARLES
Yeah. *(dreamily) (he takes a knife from the drawer)*. Listen, you'll play the husband.

MARIE
Me! He wanted to kill you with a knife?

CHARLES
Yes—you're talking about a bullfight!

64
long shot
kitchen
interior
night
music over all of
shot 64

Marie brandishes the knife and tries to trap Charles while circling around the table.

CHARLES
Not like that, not in the air. Like this, from below. Always from below. The dagger thrust

CHARLES
Not like that, not in the air. Like this, from below. Always from below. The dagger thrust.

MARIE
What should I say?

CHARLES
Nothing. Try to get me. It really was around a table.

MARIE
And Rose?

CHARLES
She was serving in the cafe. We were in the back room.

MARIE
You didn't call out?

78

CHARLES
One has one's dignity at such moments.

MARIE
And him, he didn't say anything?

CHARLES
Yes. I can still hear it: you little shit, I'll cut
you to bits.

MARIE
That rhymes: you little shit, I'll cut you to
bits. You little shit, I'll cut you to bits.

*She begins to chant as she continues to circle
around the table.*

MARIE
You little shit, I'll cut you to bits.

She rejoins Charles. He takes the arm holding the knife and the struggle ends in a dance, waltzing in time to Marie's ditty.

Scene 29

65
close shot
exterior
night

Max and Madeleine are at the fairground, at a target shooting booth. Max holds the rifle and aims.

MAX
May '68 means what to you, cherry blossom time?

MADELEINE *(she sings)*
"Cherry blossom time." And afterwards?

MAX
Afterwards? Nothing's changed.

MADELEINE
Do you think so? I'm not so sure.

MAX
Nothing's changed. Everything's worse than before. Except for the fads: the return to the land, the macro—what-do-you-call-it—food thing, the dirty children, free sex, tantrism . . . farts in a tub. Myself, I see Kissinger circling the world like a spiral. That's the hideous reality.

MADELEINE
No.

MAX
Yes.

He shoots.

Scene 30

66
long shot

A little later, they are eating grilled sausages in front of a chop-house.

exterior
night
forward track
toward them with
pan left to right to
close up of
the two

MADELEINE
You're Protestant?

MAX
No. Why?

MADELEINE
You used to be.

MAX
No. Never.

MADELEINE
When you were little your family was. You
were under the influence.

MAX
Well—O.K., possibly. But why are you
saying all this?

MADELEINE
You're a pessimist and you want actions to
produce tangible results. You're a utilitar-
ian. Me, I produce nothing. You believe in
an organized life. Soon you'll be making love
to me. You'll be thinking about morality,
even if you don't know it.

MAX
Oh? Now that's odd.

MADELEINE
You hold back or let go of your seed, it's for
practical or economic reasons, to produce
children or not. For myself, if you hold back,
that simply means that you're trying to
dissolve into the supreme void, and if you let
go you're trying to unite with the oneness of
life. You transform your religion into
morality—and me, I destroy morality
through religion.

MAX *(puzzled)*
Hold on . . . Don't you think you're complicating something that's finally pretty simple?

MADELEINE
You're doing the complicating. You divide
everything into two, good, evil, useful and
harmful. You're the court of conscience,
always judges and lawyers.

MAX *(mouth full of sausage)*
I'm all that—me?

MADELEINE
I'll go on: tantrism is the erotic game of the
cosmos in the interior of the conscience. The
whole difference is there. Max, you are
death not through roulette but through the
split into two, the masculine and the
feminine, the head and the body, the
genitals and the face. That makes you
aggressive and inflexible. Myself, I'm all one
and unique, death through fusion and disso-
lution in the universal void. There it is.

MAX
You're a little hyper. But I like you a lot.

MADELEINE
Me too, I like you a lot.

Scene 31

67
close up
interior
night

*Apartment of Mathieu and Mathilde. Evening.
Mathilde alone, is watching television. An
anonymous announcer delivers the usual news in
monotone.*

68
close up of the T.V.

ANNOUNCER
While advocating an appropriate participa-
tion I emphasize the need to reinforce coop-
eration and solidarity between employers
and workers in order to experience a true

labor peace and preserve the economic and social future of Switzerland.

Considered a progressive faction among employers, the association of young corporate leaders offers three arguments against the union initiative. It grants to union organizations, by their automatic presence in corporate life, a privilege they have no right to.

Black & White

Suddenly the announcer's tone changes. His voice becomes friendly and serious.

ANNOUNCER
Mathilde, I have something to say to you.

69
close up of Mathilde

MATHILDE
I know.

ANNOUNCER
"As far as finding a way to teach how the smallest particle of matter has been able to imprint itself with so much faith that one must consider it as the origin of life, and to determine what this faith consists of, that is the impossible thing. All one can say is that faith partakes of the essence of things and that it rests on nothing . . . "

End of Black & White

70
medium shot
interior
night

Bathroom. Mathilde is examining her belly and breasts.

71
close shot
interior
night

Her son watches her through the open door.

72
close shot
interior
night
Mathilde

MATHILDE
Tell your father I've started his beans soaking. *(she feels her belly)*

MATHILDE
Crocodile eggs!

Scene 32

73
medium shot
interior
night
light forward track

Later the same evening, Max and Madeleine are having drinks in a bar. Max calls the barmaid and offers her a banknote.

MAX
How much do I owe you?

BARMAID
Sixteen francs

MADELEINE *(she takes the banknote)*
Do you know what the origin of paper money is?

MAX
No, but that, now that interests me. I'm
learning a great deal with you today.

MADELEINE
It's the retention of feces. I always think
of that when I see De Vandoeuvres. It
makes me laugh every time.

MAX
The retention of feces?

MADELEINE
Yes, and its transformation into an economic sign of course, in gold or bills. It's
what one conceals, gold or caca. It's the
origin of the Protestant bank.

MAX
Oh? In direct contrast with many of the

other things you've said today, that seems exactly right. And that reminds me of something. A friend of mine who was studying medicine always said that he wanted to write a paper on Calvin's constipation, no less. Which held the explanation for everything.

MADELEINE
Calvin was constipated?

MAX
That's what he claimed. Constipated as a canon. Don't you find, moreover, that Geneva is a town which holds it in?

MADELEINE
Yes, I do.

Scene 33

74
medium shot
interior
night
pan left to close up
following Max
and Madeleine

Madeleine pushes the door open.

MADELEINE
"Mani padme"

MAX
Huh?

MADELEINE
It's the pass-word. To open the door.

MAX
And what does it mean?

MADELEINE
The jewel in the lotus.

MAX
Oh, O.K.

They enter. Madeleine takes off her shoes.

MADELEINE
Take your shoes off, please.

MAX
It's necessary?

MADELEINE
Yes, always.

*A moment later Madeleine, in a dressing gown,
carries in two plates of rather mysterious food
and puts them down on the mattress.*

75
medium shot
interior
night
pan showing
Madeleine entering
Indian music at the
pick-up

MADELEINE
We are going to eat. But never eat each
other. You may refuse to take off your
clothes or agree to take them off. In your
place I would agree to, it's simpler when
you're eating with your fingers. To eat
sloppily is part of the ritual. As heretical in
this domain as in others. Transgression in all
things, meat, alcohol, sex. I have some
whiskey in the kitchen. One kind of tantric
cult consisted of eating impure foods on
the naked body of a young girl, and of everyone making love together in cemeteries.

Max begins to undress

MAX
Except that you're no longer a young girl
and the cemeteries are a bit cold around here
at this time of year.

MADELEINE
Alas.

MAX
I can feel my Protestant education rushing
to the surface in a sudden billow.

They laugh

MADELEINE
Let yourself go. It will vanish in a wisp of

smoke. Have a dream and tell it to me. As for me, I'll eat. *(She takes off her dressing gown. She is naked.)*

Max leans back against the wall and closes his eyes.

76, 77, & 78
Black & White
musical chord
(percussion)

End of Black & White

Newsreel shots: fighting in the streets of Paris in May, '68

Scene 34

79
Black & White
close up, Marguerite
exterior
day, market

Marguerite cries out to the shoppers at the market.

MARGUERITE
"Noon, summer, the street is full of tomatoes, the light splits into two tomato

halves, the juice flows through the streets . . . It radiates a clear light, a benign majesty. Tragically, we must assassinate it: the knife plunges into the living pulp, it is a blood-red organ, a new sun, deep and inexhaustible."

End of Black & White

80 medium shot exterior day, market lateral track right to left on them then on to the shop- ers and back onto them in a pan	*Marcel and Marguerite are hawking their vegetables.* MARCEL Leeks! Two-fifty. Guaranteed organic. MARGUERITE Our beautiful vegetables. Get your escarole. Beautiful escarole.

Black & White

81 close up of Marguerite (idem 79)	MARGUERITE " . . . And on the table, at the summer's girdle, the tomato, fertile and recurrent earthstar, reveals its convolutions to us, its canals, its emblematic plenitude, its abundance without pits, without husk, with neither scales nor thorns. It offers us the feast of all its ardent freshness."

End of Black & White

Scene 35

82 long shot exterior day reverse track pre- ceding man from bank, then revealing Mathieu	*Vicinity of Marcel's house. Truck-gardens. Mathieu is unloading manure. A well-dressed man carrying an attaché case arrives. It's the man from the bank Max told about. He sees Mathieu and heads toward him.* MAN FROM BANK Are you Mr. Certoux?

MATHIEU
No, I am the king of shit. But if you want I
can take you to him.

MAN FROM BANK
Yes, all right.

83
close up
exterior
day

Mathieu with ironic look.

End of Reel 3

Reel 4

Scene 36

84
long shot
interior
day
kitchen

*They enter the kitchen where Marcel, Marguerite,
Zero One and the children are gathered. The
introductions are made.*

MAN FROM BANK
Did you receive our letter?

MARGUERITE
Yes, we received it.

MARCEL
We threw it out.

MAN FROM BANK
Oh? It's true one receives so much useless
paper. But it's not important since I'm here.
I'll be able to explain our project in depth to
you.

He opens his attaché case.

MAN FROM BANK
May I sit down?

MARGUERITE
Sit.

*The man from the bank sits down. The others
remain standing, except for Zero One who makes a
nuisance of himself. The man from the bank takes
out some papers.*

MAN FROM THE BANK
I assume you've already realized that the city
is expanding in your direction and I
imagine . . .

MARCEL *(cutting in)*
You want us to clear out.

MAN FROM BANK *(protesting)*
No, not at all. There's no question of that for
now. It's a matter of us examining together,

calmly, the problems you may face in a while, considering the development of the industrial zone.

The scene continues but the picture changes to black and white.

85
Black & White
close up of Marcel

MARCEL
What time do you get up in the morning?

MAN FROM BANK *(surprised)*
Me? About seven-thirty. Why?

MARCEL
And you read the ass-wipe morning paper. Around six or during the summer even earlier (he grows lyrical) one hears the birds singing. There are so many they are un- countable. As many in any case as the head- lines in the paper. They send messages

everywhere all around us. It's easy to hear them if you don't read the vile paper. But man has invented a terrible silence. Stone by stone he has constructed his own deafness and he no longer hears the messages sent forth ceaselessly around him. If he could hear them as clearly as he can hear the birds sing, he would feel a bit reassured. He doesn't have to say everything himself. And he no longer is solely responsible for keeping the world going.

86
long shot
dutch door
of the kitchen
and countryside
Music above black
and white

End of Black & White

87
close shot
interior
day
lateral track
then reverse to
close up

The same people, all seated around the kitchen table.

MARCEL
Have you ever heard a nightingale?

MAN FROM BANK
Yes, a few times.

MARCEL
From your bed?

MAN FROM BANK
Unfortunately, no. I live in the city. But in twenty years, dear Sir, your children will not be fattening on nightingales. Insofar as they can be eaten, of course.

MARCEL
Oh yes, they can be eaten.

ZERO ONE
In paté, or spitted, that's even better.

MARGUERITE
In twenty years they'll be poisoned by your chemicals.

MAN FROM BANK
I'm not in chemicals myself.

MARCEL
Some of your brothers are. And it's you who
give them the money. And to the people ex-
terminating the whales, and the ones dump-
ing mercury into the lake. I bet you don't
dare eat fish from the lake anymore.

MAN FROM BANK
But I do. People exaggerate these problems.
Fish adapt to a changing environment, as
we do.

MARCEL
Fish adapt, that's true, but your own
organism doesn't, and when you end up with
a brain full of mercury, all shriveled like
those from Minamata, well? (*he mimics*)

forward track,
returning to
close shot

MAN FROM BANK (*maintaining a smile*)
You can't accuse me of all these wrongs.

MARGUERITE (*somewhat harshly*)
Yes we can.

MARCEL
You murder the whales, you rip the ozone
from the sky, you lengthen pigs so that
they'll have two extra sets of ribs, you run
highways across the sugar-beet fields, calves
stinking of penicillin, blind chickens . . .

MAN FROM BANK (*breaks in laughing*)
Well, well! I think were straying a bit from
our subject, don't you?

MARCEL (*almost maliciously*)
You knew didn't you, that whales like music?

MAN FROM BANK
No, I didn't know that. But I also like music.

MARCEL
But you they don't murder for it.

96

ZERO ONE
I'm going to eat him.

MAN FROM BANK (*he begins to get nervous*)
What did you say?

MATHIEU
My friend says he's going to eat you.

MAN FROM BANK
Oh? All right, let's be a little serious for a
moment.

He looks for some papers.

88
long shot
same axis

MAN FROM BANK
Let's get back to our business. I'm going to
show you my little problem.

MARCEL
Uh-uh, you don't have a problem. We're
going to make a little music, since you like
that. Come on monkey-face, go to it.

*Zero One goes to get the accordion hanging from
the wall and gets set to play.*

ZERO ONE
Afterwards I'll eat him.

MARGUERITE (*very serious and firm*)
When his little piece is finished you can get
out.

*Zero One breaks into a musette-waltz. Everyone
listens seriously including the man from the bank
who keeps time.*

forward track to
close shot of Marcel,
Marguerite and man
from bank

Scene 37

89
long shot, interior
day
classroom
lateral track, then
forward toward
Mathieu, then
Marco listening, to
close up

Geneva High School. Marco's history class. Mathieu has taken the teacher's place in order to deliver the lesson on inflation. Marco sits in a corner of the classroom.

MATHIEU
. . . but crises don't fall out of the sky. Though they are obviously tied to the very structures of capitalism and its operation, one can also manufacture and provoke them. Like the fake oil crisis for example. Or organize them, stage them, as the governments of the capitalist countries are in the process of doing today in order to purge the system, eliminate the weakest and concentrate more power in the hands of the strongest . . . The recession and unemploy-

ment which come with it have both advantages and drawbacks. The advantages to the system are obvious: unemployment keeps employees in a state of fear and insecurity and therefore undemanding, and it allows for attacks from the right on our laws of society, as is happening at this time in our country. But there's a paradox here, since profit derives essentially from the surplus value taken from salaries, that is, from men's labor. They therefore agree to maintain a balance, a good reserve of unemployment, while all the time "managing" the crisis, so profitable to the great monopolies yet which like the previous one can also result in sixty million dead. For my part, I wish you luck in reaching the year two-thousand intact . . .

Black & White	*Abruptly, in the place of the twenty adolescents sitting on the benches there are more than a dozen old people.*
Brief music (percussion)	
End of Black & White	

Scene 38

90 medium shot interior day reverse track preceding Marco then lateral right to left toward the check-out counter	*Supermarket, Marco comes forward to check-out counter with his cart. Without hesitating he goes toward Marie, who rings up his purchases.*

MARIE
Four francs 30, please.

MARCO (*he had obviously added up the amount beforehand*)
Ah, there's less discrepancy than last time, but it's still off. This time I think you forgot the wine.

MARIE
I didn't forget anything. You're a pain with your fussing, you are.

MARCO
Oh, pardon me Mademoiselle.

Look of complicity from Marie

Scene 39

91
close shot
From behind, Marco
waiting. Forward
track following
him then lateral
track right to left to
close up of the two.
Music during the
waiting

*Supermarket exit. Closing time. Marco is waiting
for Marie. The employees come out. When he sees
her, Marco immediately approaches her. She is a
bit surprised.*

MARCO
I was waiting for you.

MARIE
Me?

MARCO
Well, yes. I wanted to talk to you, after what
you did for me.

MARIE
But you're not the only one I did that for. In
general its the old people, the ones barely
surviving on their pensions. With the cost of
grub, they don't go out.

MARCO
Ah, is that why they line up at your counter?

MARIE
I suppose so, yes.

MARCO
But I'm not of retirement age.

MARIE
You? I don't know, it's your head there, in
front of the check-out counter with your
forty franc whiskey.

MARCO
May I offer you a glass?

MARIE
You know, I don't have much time. I live far
away.

MARCO
Where is that?

MARIE
Across the border, near Annemasse.

MARCO
You're a border-worker?

MARIE
Yes. I have to sleep in France every night.

MARCO
Do you have a car?

MARIE
No, I take the bus.

MARCO
I'll drive you down there.

MARIE
I'm going to my friend's house. He lives
next door to me.

MARCO (*a little disapppointed*)
Well, O.K., I'll take you. If that doesn't irri-
tate your friend.

MARIE
No, it won't iritate him. What's your name?
Mine's Marie.

MARCO
Mine's Marco. My car is over there. Can I
help you with your bag?

MARIE
With pleasure.

MARCO
The pleasure is all mine.

Scene 40

92
medium shot
interior
day
corridor

A housing block near Annemasse, ten kilometers from Geneva. Apartment of Charles, Marie's friend and neighbor. They ring.

CHARLES
I'm coming. (*He goes to open the door*) Evening Marie. Ah, you're with a friend, a young man with curly brown hair. Come in.

MARIE (*to Charles*)
This is Marco. (*to Marco*)
Charles.

Charles shakes Marco's hand without much warmth.

MARCO (*surprised and reassured on seeing Charles's age*)
Glad to meet you.

103

MARIE
Marco brought me back by car.

CHARLES (*he looks at Marie's bag of groceries*)
You found everything?

MARIE
Yes, I think so.

CHARLES
All paid for?

MARIE
Almost. Not all.

CHARLES
You mustn't. You're going to get caught. I
tell you that every time. O.K., come in (*They
enter the living room*).

93
medium shot
interior
day
living room

CHARLES (*to Marco*)
She does that for you too? She does it for the
old people. She's going to get nabbed. She'll
go to prison. Are you also in canned goods?

MARCO
No, I'm a teacher.

CHARLES (*surprised*)
Oh? Have you known Marie a long time?

MARIE
Well, it must be about . . .

MARCO
A year more or less.

CHARLES
A year? And you never showed me your
fiancé?

MARIE
He didn't have a car. He lives far away.

CHARLES *(to Marie)*
You could at least have talked about him
with me. I tell you everything about myself.
(to Marco) She lives across the hall, and I
didn't even know she had a fiancé! Women
 . . . All the same she's spoken to you about
me? Engine-house Charlie?

MARCO
Oh yes, of course.

*Marie has left for the kitchen. Marco feels a little
awkward. Since there are photographs of steam
engines on the wall, he takes a chance. He indicates one of the photos.*

lateral track
right to left

MARCO
Did you drive that one? She's a beauty.

CHARLES
I drove her sister, or rather her cousin. The
most beautiful, one of the last steam jobs,
with superheating and double expansion,
which generates that kind of power through
a coupling hook . . . I had the East up there.
In the winter it wasn't very warm. It's the
241-142.

MARCO
And during the war did you drive trains?

CHARLES
In the occupied zone. I drove trains for the
krauts. Nevertheless, we managed to ar-
range a few pretty little accidents . . . Now
they pair off the German and French towns.
People have lost their memories.

MARCO
And you?

CHARLES
Me what?

MARCO
Your memory works?

CHARLES
Me? I can still hear the points screeching like it was yesterday. Every detail. Railroads interest you?

MARCO
What you know interests me. I'm a history teacher.

forward track
toward Charles
up to very close shot
Music over his
words

CHARLES
I'll tell you something, travelling by train and driving a train are two completely different things. Because of the rails. Do you still sometimes travel by train? What do you see? The countryside going by, like in the movies. Myself, I don't go to the movies anymore. But in the locomotive, the countryside doesn't go by. You travel inside. Always: inside, inside, inside. It's like a kind of music. You go in front of yourself, right to the horizon, and then it goes on, right to the place where the rails come together. And they never come together.

Scene 41

94
long shot
interior
day

Madeleine's studio. She is on the telephone.

MADELEINE
Hello Max? It's Madeleine. How are things? What are you doing right now?

95
close shot
interior
day

Max's apartment. He answers the telephone.

MAX
Right now I'm eating a small roll with jam and reading the papers. It's Sunday.

96
forward track

Madeleine's studio

106

toward Madeleine
up to very close shot

MADELEINE
And your walks to Perly-Certoux? . . . At
the bank it's caused a beautiful mess . . . I've
got the feeling it's a disaster . . . No, they
don't suspect anything. It makes me think of
you a lot. A great job. Max, I'm making two
calls at once. The first was to tell you it was a
great job. The second is a phone call of a sexual nature. It's Sunday. I'm alone. I want to
cause a silent explosion at the top of your
skull, which will open a superb lotus. I want
to stroke your vagina while you stroke my
balls *(a moment of silence)*. Are you there?

97
close up

Max's apartment.

MAX
Yes . . . I'm trying to understand. Wait a second. Aren't you mixing things up a bit? Regarding Certoux, I was just about to go see

some people down there to find out what's going on. I have to go. Maybe we could fart ourselves a lotus a little later. Silently.

Scene 42

98
very close shot of
of Max and Made-
leine from behind
in the car

A little later. In Max's car, Max taking Madeleine with him to Certoux.

MADELEINE
You didn't attach your seat-belt.

MAX
Neither did you. And what's more you're smoking.

MADELEINE
It's prohibited?

MAX
No. Not until next year.

MADELEINE
And the year after that?

MAX
The year after that there will be no more listening to the car radio.

MADELEINE
And after that?

MAX
The year after that there will be no more talking in the car.

MADELEINE
And after that?

MAX
No more dreaming. And after that, there'll be the war. Or more likely, fascism.

Scene 43

99
long shot
exterior
day
track right to left
then left to right
following move-
ments of the charac-
ters, then reverse
track and finally
forward with boom
moving from below
to above

Max and Madeleine enter the courtyard of Marcel's house. Some children playing. They stop Max.

FIRST CHILD
What's your name?

MAX
Max.

FIRST CHILD
We're going to draw you, Max.

SECOND CHILD
You're big.

MAX
Like an elephant. Since I was very small.

SECOND CHILD
We want to draw you. Over there *(he points)* against the wall.

The children take Max and stand him against the wall. Max stands motionless.

FIRST CHILD
Move! Run for your life! Take off!

Max spreads his arms and holds that position. Very precisely the children draw his outline in chalk on the wall. Mathieu who was nearby observes the children's activity very attentively. Marco and Marie enter the courtyard. They also watch.

MARCO
Hi. They've pinned you to the wall like a butterfly. *(to Mathieu)* We've been buying vegetables. *(to the group)* Let me introduce Marie.

Greetings.

MAX *(to the others)*
This is Madeleine. Lotus flower.

Mathilde arrives. Introductions.

MAX
I'm getting a cramp.

He lowers his arms.

MATHIEU
No, you wretch. Don't move. It's magnificent. Hold your pose.

Max takes the pose again. Marcel and Marguerite arrive, intrigued by the gathering. Introductions, as in formal protocol. The eight characters are gathered together for the first time. The other seven face Max, keeping his pose before the wall while the children draw.

MAX
I'm crucified.

Music with part
singing

MADELEINE *(says in English)*
It's the prophet crucified. The prophet of
'68.

MAX
It would be necessary to know whether I'm
an elephant, a butterfly or a prophet.

MARCEL
You're a bear. Did you know that bears . . .

MARGUERITE *(cuts in)*
That's it, finished.

MARCEL *(the end is sung)*
A bear marks his territory. In the forests of
Canada, bears mark their territory by making scratches on tree trunks. The bigger the
bear the higher the mark. This way the big
bear announces to the little bears that he is
bigger than they and the little bears are in
trouble.

MAX
As far as I can see is my territory. No farther.
My country only exists on a map. I'm a wet-
back, a man without a country.

MARCO
We're all border-people.

MAX
Of course, my little bear!

100
Black & White
close up
Mathieu

101
long shot of the
completed wall

*Surrounding the completed portrait of Max,
Mathieu sees the full-length portraits of Mathilde,
Marco, Marie, Marcel, Madeleine, Marguerite
and himself.*

End of Black & White

Scene 44

102 long shot exterior day	*Near the house there is a grassy embankment, made muddy by the rain. At the base of the embankment large puddles of water and mud have formed. After drawing Max on the wall, the children climbed onto the embankment to do somersaults. Then they repeatedly tumble into the mud which eventually completely covers them. Drawn by the shouting and laughter the adults have come to watch them. All eight are there and they watch in silence. No one tries to interrupt the game.*
103 *Black & White* medium shot	*Mathieu jumps in first.*
104-106 game sequence	*All the adults except for Mathilde begin to do somersaults in the same place. Soon their clothes*

Music.

End of Black & White

are coated with mud, as well as their faces and their hair.

Scene 45

107
long shot
exterior
day

Truck-gardening field. Marcel, Mathieu, Marguerite and the two zeros are at work. They are turning the ground in order to plant onions. They work hard, quickly and in silence.

108
lateral track,
right to left
close up of Margue-
rite's hands placing
onions in the ground

Scene 46

109

Bank of Geneva and Nassau. De Vandoeuvres's office. He is speaking to Marguerite whom he has summoned in order to try to persuade her.

DE VANDOEUVRES
. . . No one can resist change, you know that. Cities today are no longer what they were in the Middle Ages, certainly you agree. One can't permit the centers of cities to clog up forever. The population is growing . . .

Black & White

De Vandoeuvres' speech continues without interruption.

DE VANDOUEVRES
. . . new jobs must be found, the economy doesn't stop. And finally everything must yield to it. One goal and one duty is precisely to anticipate these changes, and to anticipate them over the long term . . .

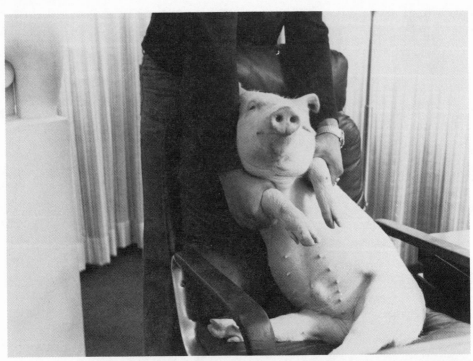

Since the start of Black and White, noises can be heard in the hallway, interjections in a foreign language, laughter. The office door opens abruptly.

110
medium shot
pan left to right
and forward track
to pig

Arrival of the two Italians.

Two immigrant workers—the ones glimpsed with Marguerite—burst into the office. They are carrying a pig in their arms. They order De Vandoeuvres coarsely to get out of his chair and they put the pig there.

111
close up of pig

End of Black & White

Scene 47

112
close shot
exterior
day

Migrant worker barracks in the area.

Marguerite is waiting on the road. A man leaves one of the barracks and comes toward Marguerite.

Workers' barracks.

ITALIAN
Your house?

MARGUERITE
No. Not today.

ITALIAN
Then somewhere else?

End of Reel 4

Reel 5

Scene 48

113
medium shot
interior
day

Marco's class at Geneva High School. The teacher's place is occupied by Marie seated on the desk. Marco is walking in the central aisle of the classroom.

lateral track right to
left to close up and
left to right
returning toward
desk

MARCO
Here is the game rule. First let me introduce Marie. Marie is a check-out girl in a supermarket. Since I am charged with giving you a history exam today and with handing out grades to you, and since neither you nor I have any desire to, I propose proceeding in the following manner: each of you by turns, but in no particular order, will ask Marie a question. And I will grade you according to the quality of your questions. I should add that Marie is a border-worker, that she is therefore obligated to sleep every night in France even though she works in Switzerland.

FIRST BOY *(to Marco)*
That annoys you, doesn't it, since you sleep in Switzerland.

Laughter.

FIRST GIRL
May I ask a small question before beginning?

MARCO
Go ahead.

FIRST GIRL
Are you in love with Marie?

MARCO
That's got nothing to do with it.

FIRST GIRL
No, but that doesn't matter.

MARCO *(after an instant's hesitation and a few glances at Marie)*
Yes, I'm in love with Marie.

A look at once astonished and satisfied from Marie.

MARCO
I'll add again that I consider it correct and justified to evaluate your knowledge of history by giving you the somewhat unusual chance to ask questions of a supermarket check-out girl who works in Switzerland and sleeps in France. Whoever wants to begin, raise your hand.

SECOND BOY
How much time does it take you to get to work?

MARIE
That depends. About an hour by bus, maybe a little more. Much less when I can find a ride.

SECOND BOY
So you hitchhike.

MARIE
Yes, sometimes. But I don't like to very much.

THIRD BOY
Why? *(to Marco)* Does it count as a question if I say simply, "Why."

Laughter.

MARCO
Explain your "why."

THIRD BOY
I mean to say: is it because of the kind of people who drive cars? In other words, you don't want the shortening of your trip to be connected with possible adventures?

MARIE
Exactly. Besides, they are not simply possible, they are inevitable.

A student puts a hand up.

THIRD BOY
Wait, I'd like to continue. What I'm asking is important. I'm tying together economic history, the supermarket, people who sleep in one country and work in another, with the history of sexuality, with the attitude of those who give a lift to Marie, that is—back to the economic—who enable her to sleep longer or have more free time against the possibility of getting felt up or even more.

Music over this

FOURTH BOY
Screwed!

THIRD BOY
That's wicked! You have no respect for people. *(to Marco)* Give him a zero.

MARCO
It's finished. Write a few pages about it for me to define your thinking.

SECOND GIRL
Marie, how much do you earn? Wait, let me be specific. With the exchange, if you live in France on a Swiss salary, do you feel that you live better than if you worked in France?

MARIE
Maybe. I don't know. In any case, I don't live well. I'm from Annecy. I would rather live in Annecy. And I don't like being a check-out girl.

Scene 48

114
long shot

Marco's apartment, evening of the same day. Marco has brought Marie home with him.

118

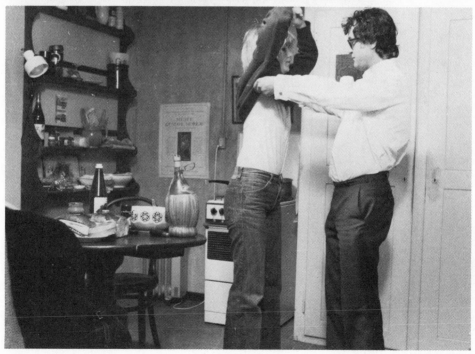

interior night Marco's kitchen	**MARCO** That's the first time I've ever made a declaration of love in public. **MARIE** It was funny. It was nice. You're going to make me break the law now. **MARCO** What law? **MARIE** The law for border-workers. I'm going to sleep on the wrong side of the border. *Marco takes off Marie's sweater. Marie unbuttons Marco's shirt.*

Scene 49

Black & White	*Marco is in a little greenhouse with a few children. He is asking them questions concerning the attribution of consciousness to things and to objects:*
115 close up Mathieu interior day	**MATHIEU** Does the wind feel the clouds? Does the bicycle know it's moving?
116 close up, Child 1	**MATHIEU** *(off camera)* Can water feel anything?
117 close up, Child 2	**MATHIEU** *(off camera)* And what if it's boiling?
118 close up, Child 3	**MATHIEU** *(off camera)* Where does the sun's name come from?
119 close up, Child 4	**MATHIEU** *(off camera)* Does it know we call it "sun"?
120 close up, Child 5	**MATHIEU** *(off camera)* When we move does the moon move with us?

121	MATHIEU
close up, Mathieu	And if we stop?
	And if we start out again in the other direction?

End of Black & White

Scene 50

122	*In the same greenhouse Mathieu, helped by the*
long shot	*children, is setting up a kind of classroom. They*
exterior	*clean, put an old mattress on the ground, an old*
day	*tarp, colored fabrics, etc.*

123	*Same scene from opposite axis*
long shot	
exterior	
day	
A few notes of music	

Scene 51

124	*Apartment of Mathieu and Mathilde. Marie, who*
medium shot	*often sleeps "on the wrong side of the border,"*
interior	*that is with their neighbor Marco, is visiting*
day	*Mathilde.*
reverse track and	
pan left to right	MARIE
	I'm exhausted and fed up. Aren't you fed up?

MATHILDE
Me too — I'm fed up.

MARIE
And besides I've got my period.

MATHILDE
I don't get them anymore.

MARIE
Oh?

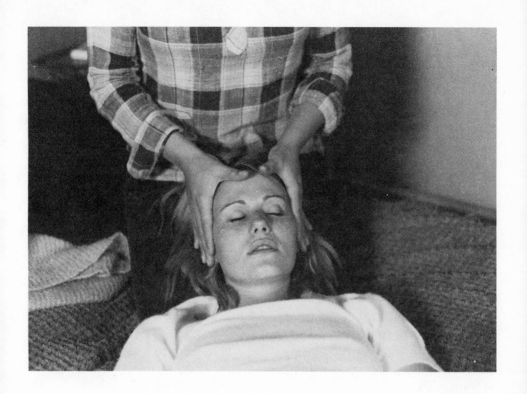

Marie is now stretched out on the couch and Mathilde is very skillfully massaging her temples.

125
close up
Marie's face and
Mathilde's hands

A little later, Marie asleep on the couch.

126
medium shot
Marie sleeping
Musical chord
over 126

Scene 52

127
long shot

Supermarket. Marie at her check-out stand. A little farther off two plain-clothes police inspectors

interior
day
forward track
toward check-out
counter, then lateral
left to right
following the police
inspectors and
forward toward the
store following the
pursuit

*along with the manager of the store come rapidly
toward Marie. One of them takes out his police
identity card.*

FIRST INSPECTOR
Will you please follow us, Miss.

MARIE
Follow you where?

FIRST INSPECTOR
Into my office. I have some questions to ask
you.

MARIE
Fuck off.

FIRST INSPECTOR
Come on, come on, don't make a scene. Your
case is serious enough as it is.

Music at end linking
with 128

*Abruptly Marie leaves her station and runs for it.
The inspectors follow her and cut off her exit.
Marie then sets off in the direction of the store
where the inspectors catch up with her and grab her
between two rows filled with preserves. Marie in-
sults them, cries out and argues.*

MARIE
You bastards! You bastards!

Scene 53

128
long shot
exterior
day, greenhouse
forward track to
medium shot of
Mathieu giving a
mathematics lesson

MATHIEU
Fourteen. O.K., now fifteen? Frank?

CHILD
Yes.

MATHIEU
Is it a multiple of three?

CHILD
Yes.

124

MATHIEU
Why?

CHILD
Because it's . . .

MATHIEU
Right. Now eighteen, Cecile.

CHILD
Uh, in the middle.

MATHIEU
Here? There?

CHILD
Yes.

MATHIEU
Is it a multiple of two?

CHILD
Yes.

MATHIEU
Is it an even number?

CHILD
Yes.

MATHIEU
Is it a multiple of three?

CHILD
Yes.

MATHIEU
Then that's it for eighteen?

Scene 54

129
close shot
lateral track right to
left following Marcel
and Marguerite
then reverse track as
they move off at the
end of the scene

Marcel and Marguerite, who don't yet know about the "school," have seen something through the panes of glass. Mathieu comes out of the greenhouse to join them.

MARGUERITE
What's going on in there?

MATHIEU
You can see—I'm growing flowers. It's the ideal place.

MARGUERITE
But they're supposed to be in school now!

MATHIEU
And in fact they are.

MARGUERITE
What's all this about?

MARCEL
You're playing the schoolmaster now, in a greenhouse?

126

MATHIEU
Yes, as you can see. They like it a lot.

MARGUERITE
And how long has this circus been running?

MATHIEU
For two days.

MARGUERITE
And the work?

MATHIEU
I arranged it with the Zeros. Everything'll be fine. And I'll get them to help with some of the easy jobs. *(He indicates the children)*

MARCEL
Them?

MATHIEU
Sure, them. Why not?

MARGUERITE
But if they don't go to school, we'll be asked questions. It's mandatory. You're a little nuts. We're going to end up with the cops here.

MATHIEU
It's not school that's mandatory, it's educating the children. That's what I'm doing.

MARCEL
That's not your trade.

MATHIEU
I'm working on it. Each evening. It's no joke. Everything will go well, you'll see. Even the lousiest inspector wouldn't find anything to beef about here.

MARGUERITE
Says you! You're going to stop this circus. It's just not possible.

MATHIEU
No. At least wait to see how it goes before deciding. You're not the only one to decide.

MARGUERITE *(going away) (off camera)*
We've already had enough problems like that. More business about kids not going to school.

Scene 55

130
medium shot
interior
day
lateral track left to
right on Marco who
is walking in the aisle

Marco's class at Geneva High School. History lesson.

MARCO
What have you got for me today? No one wants to speak? You're dozing. If it will help, try to tie up what I've just told you with your own experience and your own desires. May-

be that will give you an answer, or bring you closer to one.

FIRST BOY
And what if we don't want to talk about our desires. What if we decide that they're personal and secret?

MARCO
That's not what I'm asking you for.

FIRST GIRL
Yes it is.

SECOND BOY
Tell us first about yours, about your desires.

THIRD BOY
That's right. Why do we have to talk about our desires and not you?

MARCO
Now we're getting away from the subject.

SECOND GIRL
If I ask you now, at this moment, what your desire is, would you agree to answer?

MARCO
It's that you stop dozing off.

FIRST BOY
Not true.

FIRST GIRL
Your secret desire, right now. We won't be shocked, you know.

SECOND BOY
Go ahead!

SEVERAL STUDENTS
Your desire, M'sieur, go ahead!

SEVERAL STUDENTS
Your secret desire! Tell the truth! The truth!

Shouts, laughter, beating on tables.

SECOND GIRL
What are you thinking about at this moment? About Marie!

SEVERAL STUDENTS
About Marie!

MARCO
With this kind of noise, I don't see what I could think about.

FOURTH BOY
Quiet! Let him think.

Complete silence.

FOURTH BOY
He's thinking. About Marie?

MARCO *(amused)*
If that's what you want. About Marie or maybe someone else as well.

THIRD GIRL
Who?

MARCO
My secret desire is one time to go to bed with
two women. Are you happy?

A brief musical   *The students laugh and shout.*
chord over the end

Scene 56

131   *In Marcel's kitchen. Marco, Max and Mathieu*
medium shot   *are preparing dinner together. They are making*
interior   *an onion tart. Mathieu is making the crust. Max is*
night   *cutting the onions and Marco is frying them in a*
focuses on the   *pan.*
kitchen

MARCO
I got myself sacked by the school.

MATHIEU
Anything else would have amazed me. What
are you going to do to eat?

MARCO
Well . . . But I think I've found new work.
For the time being.

MAX
Where?

MARCO
In an old people's home.

MAX
Huh? Doing what?

MARCO
Because they're rejected. They get stuck
with a label, "citizens—stage three," in order
to shove them aside. We've got to make them
revive a bit, move around, talk, sing.

MAX
All you're doing is playing with the number
three. You must be confusing the third stage
with the third world.

132
close up, onions,
pan right to left
then vertical on
Mathieu's face
All of the following
scene in pans alter-
nating left to right
and right to left
across the three
faces
Music over first
part of 132

MATHIEU *(he chants)*
The onion is a superb and democratic vegetable. It grows everywhere. It has a tough
skin to protect it from the cold. It flavors
everything. It lasts. You can eat it raw or
cooked. It's sweet and a little bitter too. It
kills germs. It's cheap.

MARCO
I'd vote for cabbage myself.

MAX
All manner of virtue in vegetables. Eat your
vegetables! So you're going to retire to an old
people's home? And become a kind of leek?

MATHIEU
The tart would be better if we had a wood
stove.

MAX
Always the past! A wood stove! The little old
people! Next time you'll arrive in a horse and
buggy.

MARCO
Where you're way off is in thinking that
revolution is made for the future. Revolution is the revenge of the past. You see dawn,
I see an old tree. And so?

MAX
You're in reverse. Because we live in a time
of disillusionment you're in reverse. Everyone's looking for an escape-hatch, the body,
nature, sex, onions, the lotus flower. All the
little consolations in order to escape from an
intolerable world said to be unchangeable.

MATHIEU
You don't sanction the little pleasures?

MAX
Little pleasures. Everything's little. Little
tricks, little schemes. *(to Marco)* With the kids
you could have influenced the future if you
hadn't gotten yourself sacked, you little
smart-ass.

MARCO
I could only undermine the present. It's not
the same thing, you big smart-ass.

MAX
Subvert the present to build the future.
Exactly what I said.

MARCO *(he has tears in his eyes from the onions)*
One must always sacrifice oneself for the
future. Bullshit. That's the big con-game of
revolutions. Come to that, it's also what capitalism has always preached. In fact, it's you
who live in the past. What you're waiting for
is another 1905, 1917 or 1968.

MAX
What will you be able to teach the old folks?
Nothing.

MARCO
You'd rather I taught dates to high school
students?

MAX
I simply wish you'd teach them that capitalism can collapse.

MARCO
Already did it. And got canned for it. Out
you go!

133
medium shot
forward track
towards Marco in
front of the sink
then pan right to left
toward the table
where he returns to
to sit

MATHIEU
You talk and talk, and you're both a pain in
the ass. In fact it's simple, you work to earn a
living. With the surplus of energy that remains some of us fight the profit-making
system. It's simple.

MAX
Utterly simple. Just like that. Utterly simple,
utterly little, utterly littler and littler.

MARCO
With the old folks I can be crazy.

MATHIEU
If I was old I'd like you a lot.

MAX
I hope I never get old.

MARCO
So bump yourself off. Me, I'm already old.
(The onion tears run down his cheeks.) And that's
why I can see clearly. Old people take time
for what it is, because they have so little of it.
Having a lot makes you believe that time is
the future and the past. Of course, their present is full of memories of the past. All the
world's memories are in the present. And all
its hopes too. But these memories and hopes
are a creation of the present and not what
destroys it. That's why I like old people
and want to play with them.

MAX
In ten years you'll be fed up with your little
games.

MARCO
And you with roulette.

MAX
·I'm no hero. I've dropped out but I refuse to
shrivel up. Someday you'll be forced to recognize that some people—and I hardly
include myself—were right to make priorities and stick to them.

MARCO
But you'll have waited so long that you'll
have gotten dangerous.

MAX
I certainly hope so.

MARCO
I mean dangerous to your little comrades.
Big smart-ass.

Scene 57

134
close up, Mathilde,
interior
night

*Marcel's kitchen. Nearing the end of the meal.
Everyone is there together, except for Marie who is
in prison. The children do the serving with playful
ceremony.*

MATHILDE
I have something to announce. To everyone.

135
long shot, kitchen
forward track to full
full close-up of
characters and circle
around table
reverse track to
return of long shot
at end of scene

MARGUERITE
You're pregnant.

MATHILDE
How did you know that? Did Mathieu tell
you?

MATHIEU
I haven't told anyone.

MARGUERITE
I sorted it out.

MARCEL
Marguerite is a sorceress, don't forget. She
reads the stars and spiderwebs.

MATHILDE
Nothing shows. He's three months old. It's
Mathieu who told you.

MARGUERITE
No. I sorted it out. From your head.

MATHILDE
How? It's visible? I've got marks?

MADELEINE
No, but it shows anyway.

MATHILDE
How come? There's some look about me?

MATHIEU
You have the look of someone pregnant. I
see it too. In the eyes.

MARCEL
It's in your manner.

MARCO
You're big. Big Mathilde.

MAX
Enormous Mathilde.

MADELEINE
Superb Mathilde. It's true, the kid is coming
through your eyes.

MATHILDE
It's a boy.

MARCO
Or else a girl.

MATHIEU
No, a boy.

MAX
The poor thing!

MARCO
I'm leaning toward a girl. I'll bet.

MATHILDE
It's a boy. I'll bet. I'm sure of it.

MARCO
Is there some trick to knowing?

MATHILDE
Yes.

MATHIEU
It's a matter of technique.

MARGUERITE
Explain it to us.

MATHILDE
Explaining it isn't easy.

MADELEINE
It's a position.

MAX
Standing on your head, toes in the shape of a
lotus.

MARCO
It's a special trick?

MATHIEU
Yes. Actually not so special.

MATHILDE
Simple.

MAX
I know. It's the missionary position. In
effect, simple. It will be a simple boy. A sim-
pleton. He'll be a missionary.

MARCO
I don't believe in your trick at all. I'll bet on a
girl. She'll be called Marie.

MADELEINE
Marie? Why?

MARCO
Because of Marie who isn't here. Marie-in-
prison. She'll be called Marie.

MAX
Marie, that's a bit of Jesus-Mary.

MARGUERITE
Three months now. Birth at the beginning
of autumn. Libra. A girl, ladies and gentle-
men. A rose. Rose-Marie to please Marco. Or
Rosemonde, rose of the world. Her first husband will be the moon. And you Mathilde,
what name do you want?

MATHILDE
Me? I don't have one. Just yet. Later.

MAX
Mine is Leo.

MADELEINE
What? Leo! That's awful.

MATHIEU
Why Leo?

MAX
Leo because of Leo. There aren't exactly a
lot of them around.

MATHIEU
Mine is Emile. Because of Jean-Jacques.

MATHILDE
Emile, Leo. You're all nuts.

MAX
Madeleine, your turn. Go ahead.

MADELEINE
No, I've no idea. Or very simply Shiva, or
Shakti.

MAX
Very simply.

MARCEL
Who are they?

MADELEINE
They're the one and the other. He and she.
Shiva or Shakti, Shakti or Shiva, or the two
together. All beings are double, male and
female with one side dominant. Why place
them in opposition? Why wish for a boy?

MAX
So that he can take over the business.

MADELEINE
He'll be nothing, the great void of love, the

abolition of duality, the return to the one. He was made in a moment which is at once the most intense affirmation of time and its negation, the union of being and the void. Two in one, the lotus and the lightning, the vulva and the phallus, the right hand and the left . . .

MAX *(cutting in)*
The owners and the workers, the exploiters and the exploited. Everything equals everything. Nothing exists anymore.

MADELEINE
What a bastard that one is. Look, you're about to make me cry.

In fact she is near tears.

Zero One enters the kitchen with his accordion, sits in a corner and begins to play.

MARCO
There's still Marcel who hasn't said anything.

MARCEL
Mathilde is right. It's a boy. He'll be called Jonah. I've always thought that Mathilde resembled a whale.

MATHILDE
A whale! Thank you!

MARCEL
In spirit of course. I'm making you a wonderful compliment. No one can blame the whales for anything. Mathilde, Jonah is going to come. He fell from the ship, from the beautiful ship of fools we navigate on. He jumped into the water and you swallowed him because you're nice. You saved his life and now you're going to spit him out. That's him. That's Jonah!

Piano accompaniment to accordion, and song

MATHIEU
Jonah. Not bad.

MARCO *(he sings)*
In the year 2000 Jonah will be twenty-five.
In twenty-five years the century will spit him out.

MAX
Or rather puke him up.

MARCO *(he sings and the others join in)*
The whale of history will spit out Jonah who will be twenty-five in the year 2000. That's the time left for us to help him get off the shit-pile.

End of Reel 5

Reel 6

Scene 58

Caption: "A Year Later"

136   *Whales at sea*
close up
Black & White
a musical chord

End of Black & White

Scene 59

137
long shot of
Mathilde's face as
she nurses Jonah

142

138
long shot of the new-
born Jonah nursing
at his mother's breast

Scene 60

139
medium shot
interior
day

Charles's apartment. Marie enters with a basket of provisions.

CHARLES
Thank you, Marie. All paid for, I hope?

MARIE
Yes. Here's the receipt, chief.

140
long shot
kitchen

Charles is cleaning vegetables at the table. Marie washes them at the sink.

CHARLES
Did you find work?

MARIE
No.

CHARLES
You don't have to tell them about your past.
How are you going to live?

MARIE
I'm moving in with Marco.

CHARLES
You can't. It's on the other side of the
border. They'll nab you again. It's called
violating parole.

MARIE
I'll stay out of sight. At this point I don't feel
much like moving around.

CHARLES
Nonetheless you've got to do something.

MARIE
Why? Do what? Sit at a cash-register or on
an assembly line—that's the same thing as
being inside, and you don't even keep track
anymore.

141
long shot
kitchen
kitchen from other
axis, after the
meal

CHARLES
Marie, I want to play. We haven't played for
months.

MARIE
I wasn't able to. I wouldn't have been able
to. I thought I was going a little crazy.

CHARLES
But we are a little crazy.

He goes to get his locomotive fireman's goggles.

MARIE
No, not the train. And not the trip. Prison.

CHARLES
Prison?

She leaves the kitchen and goes into the sitting room.

pan left to right on
Charles who
follows her

MARIE
Yes, prison.

CHARLES
All right. So you're in your cell. What do
I do?

MARIE
You're someone I'm thinking of.

CHARLES
Who?

MARIE
Up to you.

Charles goes to a corner of the room and pretends to be pissing.

MARIE
No. You have to be a woman.

CHARLES
Why?

MARIE
I saw only women for six months.

CHARLES
You saw the chaplain didn't you? That gives
me an idea.

142
long shot on the
other axis

He leaves the room. The door to the toilet can be heard opening. He returns with a piece of toilet paper around his neck. She sits stiffly erect in the middle of the room. He pretends to knock on the door.

MARIE
No. There's no knocking. You come in like a doctor entering a hospital room.

CHARLES (*he enters*)
My child, I'm going to tell you the story of the fat wine-maker and the gallant peasant.

MARIE
You haven't got it at all. The chaplin wasn't an old fruitcake. He was young. Every time he was there I'd imagine him making love.

She hits him on the chest.

MARIE
You rot in there, you rot!

CHARLES
I can play a woman, or the pastor. Or what else?

MARIE
There wasn't anyone else.

CHARLES (*he draws himself erect, covering his face with his hands*)
I'll be the door to the cell. I'm a female guard watching you.

He opens his fingers and peers surreptitiously through them.

CHARLES
She's left.

He closes his fingers. Marie rises and goes to strike Charles's hands. He reopens his fingers to peer surreptitiously once more and cries out.

short forward track

CHARLES (*imitating a woman's voice*)
Stop that trouble-making little bitch!

MARIE
You don't know what it's like to be locked up. You don't know!

146

She collapses in tears.

Scene 61

143
long shot
interior
day. Kitchen
forward track to
close shot
of Marguerite

*Kitchen of Marcel's house. Marguerite and
Madeleine are working together to prepare the
pamphlet Marguerite is collaborating on.
Madeleine types up the pages. Marguerite
mimeographs them.*

MADELEINE
Do I have to list all the chemical additives
they put in the salad?

MARGUERITE
Yes. That makes a big impression. And we
have to get a move on if we want to get the
pamphlet out by next week.

147

MADELEINE
But there are twenty-seven additives.

MARGUERITE
I know.

MADELEINE
They've all got Chinese names. All twenty-seven go into the same salad?

MARGUERITE
Yes.

Scene 62

144
long shot
interior
day. Common room
forward track
during singing up to
close shot of Marco

Rest home for old people. In a common room Marco sits at the piano and rehearses a song with about ten old people. The song is "Cherry Blossom Time."

MARCO (*singing alone at first*)
When we sing of cherry blossom time
the mocking birds and nightingales
will all be glad.

The old people join in together.

The beautiful girls will go a bit mad
and lovers' hearts will shine.
When we sing of cherry blossom time
the mocking birds will whistle along.

Piano music added
over last stanza

But cherry-blossom time too soon is gone
when two gather flowers and dream as one.

Scene 63

145
Black & White
close shot
interior
night
End of Black & White

Marco's apartment. Bedroom. Marco in bed with Marie and an unidentified girl.

148

146
medium shot then
forward track to
close up of Marco
and pan to close up
of Marie

*Marco's kitchen. Marco and Marie are having
dinner. Water can be heard running in the
bedroom.*

MARIE
Why did you want to go to bed with
two women?

MARCO
I don't know. Everyone wants to at least
once. It's a fantasy.

MARIE
Well tonight it isn't a fantasy anymore.

MARCO
No.

*He is at the same time both pleased and a little
disturbed.*

MARCO
Is she going to stay in the bathroom for long?

MARIE
She's washing her hair.

MARCO
Why was she in prison?

MARIE
She stole. That's all.

MARCO
Is she really terrific?

MARIE
Listen, since you left it up to me, I wouldn't bring you a dog, huh? And it's only this once. You promised.

MARCO
Sure, it's a deal. Still I would rather have seen
her first . . . Those nights in prison must
have been long.

MARIE
No. The nights were short. It's evenings that
are long. There are girls who talk about
nothing else. They get worked up and then
they masturbate. Some become lesbians.
Inside. Probably not once they're out.

MARCO
Does she shack up?

MARIE
Yes. At first I couldn't accept it. Later, it's
different than you imagined.

147
medium shot
interior
night
bedroom then
circular track
around bed to full
change of axis
Music over camera
movement

*A little later. Marco and Marie are sitting face
to face on the bed, naked.*

MARIE
It's funny how someone can change when
you touch their sex. When you take away
your hand it's over, it goes back to the
way it was. That must be the difference when
you love someone. You stay the same before
and after.

MARCO
Your pal is taking a long time.

MARIE
She's coming.

Louise enters the room.

Scene 64

148
long shot
interior
day

*Mathieu's class in the greenhouse. Mathieu plays
Marcel's record for the children, the song of the
whales recorded underwater.*

151

greenhouse

MATHIEU
I'm going to play this song of the whales for you, recorded underwater. I'll hang the first one who talks.

Fade to black

149
fade opens up frame
by frame

Repeat of the song of the whales. The children imitate the voices.

Scene 65

150
medium shot
exterior
day. Courtyard wall
reverse track when
Marguerite moves
away from the wall

The children from Mathieu's class have "pinned" Marguerite and Marcel against the courtyard wall in order to draw them. Mathieu looks on very satisfied. On the wall there are already six people, Max, Madeleine, Mathieu, Mathilde, Marguerite Marie, all shining with brilliant colors.

152

Musical chords over
the camera move-
ment

MARGUERITE
Will it last long?

MATHIEU
As long as it has to.

MARGUERITE
Hurry it up a bit. I've got something else to
do.

MATHIEU
Not right now. You haven't got anything else
to do. Nothing better anyway.

MARGUERITE
There are my carrots.

MARCEL
Her carrots.

MATHIEU
Your carrots will make out all right for five
minutes without you.

MARGUERITE (*she moves away from the wall*)
You think so?

MATHIEU
What are you doing? Stay there!

MARGUERITE
I've had it.

MATHIEU
Stay there! They have to finish!

MARGUERITE
Then they'll finish without me.

MATHIEU
That's impossible. Go back to your place.

MARGUERITE
No.

MATHIEU
Go back to your place, I'm telling you. All the
others did it.

MARGUERITE
No. You give me a pain in the ass with that
stuff. I've got work to do.

MATHIEU
Five minutes. It's important. Let them finish.

MARGUERITE
Finish what? What's so important? Your
fucking around doesn't seem so important
to me.

MATHIEU
What do you mean?

MARGUERITE
I'm not paying you in order to get drawn on
a wall. I don't give a fuck about your wall. It's
been a year since you did anything around
here.

MATHIEU
I'm working with the kids.

MARGUERITE
I didn't hire you for that. I hired you to carry
the shit. Your school's costing me too much.
No one goes outside anymore.

MARCEL (*conciliatory*)
It's true Mathieu. We're paying you and
everyone stays inside.

MATHIEU
They're your kids too, aren't they?

MARGUERITE
They can to to school like all the others.

MATHIEU
No.

MARGUERITE
Yes.

MATHIEU
They get screwed up at school.

MARGUERITE
Didn't you go yourself. And me? And
Marcel? That didn't fuck us up any worse.
Everyone stays inside. I pay school taxes on
one hand and then I pay again on the other.
It's not possible any more.

MATHIEU
That's what you think!

MARGUERITE
Do you want to check the books? You wanted
to check them so badly. So come and look.
It's impossible to do everything—pay to get
rid of the chemicals and pay for your school.

MATHIEU
I don't give a damn about your books. What's
more important, your kids or some carrots?

MARGUERITE
The kids will manage.

MARCEL
So you just tell the kids—Clear out—and
then they'll manage.

MATHIEU
Pigs do exactly the same thing. Are you pigs?

MARGUERITE
Pigs or not, tomorrow my kids go to school.
Not yours, the other. And you go back to
work. I'm not going to pay you anymore for
doing nothing.

MATHIEU
Out of the question.

MARGUERITE
Yes. It's decided.

MATHIEU
You don't decide for me. I'll go do something else.

MARGUERITE
As you wish. Give me your answer tomorrow
morning.

*She moves off, returning to the house. The voices
grow louder.*

MATHIEU
You've got it now. Find someone else for
your shit and ship your kids to the slaughter-
house. And I'll keep the apartment,
Comrade Landlady. For Jonah.

*Marguerite is already far away. She is almost
crying.*

MARGUERITE (*off camera*)
Keep it if you want. For Jonah. And go fuck
yourself!

Caption: A Month Later

Scene 66

151
medium shot
interior
day. Kitchen
reverse track and
pan left to right
toward Mathieu

Some time later. Mathieu's apartment. He finishes
his breakfast and gets ready to go to work.
Mathilde and the children are with him but not
yet dressed.

MATHILDE
How many workers are there?

MATHIEU
Around a hundred. Maybe more.

MATHILDE
It's really awful.

MATHIEU
Yes. The job's fucked.

MATHILDE
All the same you should check at the print
shop.

MATHIEU
No. I don't want to print anything any more.

MATHILDE
It's not warm out. You're going to die of cold
on the motorbike.

MATHIEU
Right. Fine.

Scene 67

152
close shot
exterior
day
reverse track
preceding Mathieu
on his motorbike

*Mathieu is going to work on his motorbike.
He's passing through the suburbs.*

MATHIEU (*he chants*)
Oh Marguerite the sorceress, Oh Marco the
philosopher, Oh Marie the thief, Oh Marcel
the hermit, Oh Max the former prophet,
Oh Madeleine the madwoman.

153
medium shot
lateral track
left to right

Mathieu on his motorbike.

MATHIEU (*voice-over*)
I want to try to tie the threads of your desires
together so that they won't scatter. I'm
returning to work. I'll be exploited. I'll try to
tie it together, to unify the field of your
desires so that they'll function as crow-bars.
I'm cold.

154
long shot
exterior
full day. Suburbs
long high-angle
shot on cross-roads
where Mathieu
arrives

Mathieu stops at a red light.

MATHIEU (*voice-over*)
I am in the twentieth century, Jonah. All
they ask is simply that I accept everything
quietly. I can't touch the goods they pay me
for. I'm manual labor, manual labor on my
bike.

155
close shot

Mathieu waiting.

156
long reverse angle
shot with red light
and bank

157
close up of Mathieu

MATHIEU
Goddamn fucking ass-hole red light.

158
close up of red light
going out

159
long shot
extreme high-angle
shot of suburb

text off over
Mathieu in black
and white

MATHIEU (*voice, off camera*)
It's cold early this morning. I'm also thinking about the warmth of my bed. Jonah, the game's not up. Let's take it from the moment when you learn to walk.

Right to the one when the police and the army fire on thousands like you. From your first reading lesson right up to the final democratic decison: to yield nothing more whatever the danger.

160
Black & White

Newsreel, Geneva 1932. Crowd of workers.

161
Black & White
Musical chord
(percussion over
black and white)

Arrival of soldiers by truck.

162
Black & White

Armed soldiers in front of military barracks.

163
End of Black & White

Armed soldiers containing the crowd.

Scene 67 (sequel)

164
long shot
exterior
day. Reverse track
following Mathieu
on his motorbike

MATHIEU (*voice-over*)
Will things be better for you? The best are systematically discarded.

165
close up
exterior, day
lateral track right
to left following
Mathieu
Musical theme
(piano) over 165

MATHIEU (*voice-over*)
I'll say: no one's going to make decisions for us anymore. The first time maybe nothing will happen, the tenth there'll be a committee, the hundreth time a strike and the hundred and first time, another reading lesson for you, Jonah. As many times as I'll get on my bike to go to work. No, more: as many times as the days of my life.

Scene 68

166
long shot
interior
day
tobacconist

Max comes in to tobacconist.

MAX
Gauloise filters please.

THE SALESGIRL (*she gives him a pack*)
Two-thirty, please.

MAX
Two-thirty? Yesterday they were still two-
ten.

SALESGIRL
Everything's going up. It's inflation.

Max pays and leaves.

Caption: A Day in 1980

Scene 69

167
Black & White
exterior
day, close shot
of statue of
Jean-Jacques
Rousseau

VOICE (*off-camera*)
" . . . needs change according to men's
situations. There is truly a difference
between the man of nature living in a state
of nature and the man of nature living in
society. Emile is not a primitive to be con-
signed to the wilderness. He is a primitive
made for living in the city."

Scene 70

168
long shot
exterior, day
Forward track with
movement of crane
lowering toward the
wall, then pan left
to right on the eight
characters
Music (cello solo)
over 168

The courtyard of Marcel's farm.

MATHILDE'S VOICE (*off-camera*)
Jonah! Jonah!

*Jonah raises his head but stays in the courtyard.
The camera advances and descends toward him,
then leaves him and approaches the eight
"prophets" drawn head to foot on the grey wall of
the courtyard. Despite the years and the elements,
the brilliant colors have survived, even though
sections of the drawings are beginning to
disappear.*

169
close shot
still of
Jonah drawing

Final credits
over end

End of Reel 6

An Interview with Alain Tanner

Cahiers: What seem to me to come the most into play for the spectator are pleasure and astonishment (laughter): pleasure because you recognize yourself there, and astonishment that you recognize yourself. This seems to be the first time such "marginal" practices have been employed. But doesn't their marginality register not only in relation to the dominant system but also in relation to the actual "legacy of '68"? How do you locate these practices within the whole dispute?

What do you think of the way this "legacy" (characters + marginal practices) enters present French cinema?

Also: Why Geneva, Switzerland, the frontier: How do you explain that only Godard, Reusser and you manage to film leftism?

A. Tanner: This pleasure derives in effect from a certain complicity between spectator and characters, from the fact that "they discover themselves there." But insofar as a large number of spectators are situated outside the activities of these characters (in Switzerland *Jonah* played to a public far larger than this milieu), I think the thread of pleasure must extend further back. it must extend to a complicity with the film itself, with the mode of discourse (even if the audience isn't entirely conscious of it) and with the particular practices of those of us who made the film, and finally, tying it together, with our particular pleasure in organizing and working on this material in this way. This is something of a wager, but I don't think I'm mistaken and I attach a lot of importance to this notion in the case of *Jonah.*

It's accurate to observe that the marginality of the characters locates itself where one doesn't expect it, at the same time that it's ambiguous with regard to the situation of these characters. They are marginal "from the inside." If you were to trace a circle which would contain the social body, they would certainly be situated at the margin, but that margin is within the circle. The wind pushing the cast-offs of '68 always blows toward the exterior, toward the outside. We wanted to reverse the flow so that the seeds it carries would fall within. Hence ambiguity. We didn't want to hold up a mirror for this or that group so that they could crowd in to admire themselves. The extreme radicals don't discover themselves there, and they are often the most mediocre interpreters of the film: they "learn nothing" obviously (and above all not how to look at images); I "offer no solutions," etc. . . . The characters therefore are not "drop-outs." They are bound to the circle if only by their work, all the while refusing to allow themselves to be drawn toward its center. It's the poison in their blood. A slow poison, of course, but that's the proposition of the film. Switzerland? Geneva? The frontier? I live there. I work there. That's all. It's true we are somewhat pedagogical around here, and natural that Rousseau would serve as patron for one of our stories. If in additon we speak of certain things which French film obscures, it's probably because here it's we who have made the film beginning from zero, outside of any context and any cultural, industrial or commercial tradition, beyond the open or hidden pressures which weigh more heavily elsewhere. But you lose nothing by waiting and you have to open your eyes. Also, the total lack of means at the start forced us to concentrate on the meaning rather than spectacle and atmosphere.

Cahiers: You said yourself in the interview with *Libération* that you neglected a number of these "marginal," "subversive" practices "of reorientation." Are there any others you would like to discuss? Do you think priorities should be established among these practices that one can still argue for in terms of "tactics" and "strategies"?

A. Tanner: John Berger and I didn't "neglect" certain practices of reorientation, we left them aside. We didn't want to establish an inventory or a catalogue. Also we wanted to avoid overly fixed discourses, in order to remain within the circle. The choice was made little by little considering what was nearest to us as well as photos of the eight actors who formed the departure point for elaboration of the scenario. Therefore the "strategy" is more concerned with the film, its discourse and its audience than with reality.

Cahiers: You also said that you deliberately chose to treat the film as a "fable," to reject systematically any realistic reading. Is that generally an option for you, or did the subject call for it? And don't you have the impression that your fable confronts (goes beyond) a kind of realism (to be redefined in relation to "bourgeois" realism), which would be that of (collective) desire? One really gets the feeling of being there and not being there, in reality, in fiction.

A. Tanner: I have always tried to reject realistic writing and reading. It's true by contrast that I call on certain relevant elements from the "classical" code of repesentation: a feeling of the real, for example recognizable characters. But these elements only appear within the strict limits assigned to them—in the guise of reference points for the audience. They are precisely circumscribed within the little "pieces" of the film, inside the scenes, but they never operate at the level of total structure. Looking a little closer, despite the eruption of "realism," of the "lived," of recognizable characters (but with whom one can't identify), if finally everything rings false in *Jonah* it's because the filming effects a distortion of the representational mode. It dismantles the mechanism and plays with it even when it issues from it. This derives not only from the non-linearity of the story, but above all from the internal structure of each scene (see the shot-sequence). If the redefinition of realism did proceed that way, through what you call the "realism of desire," I would feel I had moved a step forward. And when you also say "that one has the feeling of being there, in reality, in fiction," you put your finger precisely on the question. To me it's obvious, but it's the first time a critic has said it. This push-pull movement between the attraction of the real and the uncoupling from the real, between the "true" and the "false," is the basis of my work on writing and fiction. To disengage each time the fiction gets into gear permits the spectator to catch the ball on the first bounce and prohibits him from burying himself in his semi-conscious state. It gives him back his place and establishes the dialogue.

Cahiers: The actors really seem to make the film, and you didn't choose just anyone. What do they stand for in relation to the new generation of comic actors, and what do you see as the "direction of actors"? . . .

A. Tanner: The actors: the starting point of the film, beyond simply beginning to pay real attention, was the definitive and radical choice of eight actors (who only learned of it six months later). Eight because ten was too many and six not enough. Pairs because men and women. The actors "inspire" the film more than they make it. With this method there is, upstream from the film, a whole background which results in the fact that the actors' work at the moment of filming is nothing more than a kind of "precipitate." The "direction of the actors" becomes a mold, part of a procedure which traces back to a year of filming. The characters no longer elude me, except through the accident of imponderable factors or moods. Morever, it's evident that in *Jonah* the actors belong to a kind of "family." If I'm not mistaken, it's François Truffaut who distinguished between "poetic" actors and "psychological" actors. By instinct I'm drawn to the former. The rest is a matter of work and sometimes patience, but there is no "method" to impose, insofar as they already have their own, which sometimes consists of not having one, but which in any case is never the same from one to another.

Cahiers: There are very beautiful shot-sequences in the film, particularly the one of the "onions," where the camera in turn shoots the three men "talking politics" while cooking. Does this refusal of shot-reverse shot correspond with a precise purpose of yours?

A. Tanner: The entire film is structured through use of the shot-sequence. Each scene is constituted solely from a shot (150) and the minimal cutting only intervenes in the case of a few intercut close-ups, except in the case of absolute technical necessity or deficiencies of the actors vis-à-vis the text. There are fewer than ten movement and time splices through the entire film, and these are definitely "bad" splices. Much could be said about the shot-sequence; it's a problem which leads back to many others. There isn't the space or the time. I'll try to summarize.

a) It is inaccurate to claim that the shot-sequence only hypnotizes the spectator and facilitates his manipulation by supplementing the effect of the real. It is rather cutting which produces this effect and of course the recomposing of the scene through "invisible" montage. This is where the classic narrative codes locate, since above all this technique facilitates erasure of all traces of the work. The camera is a heavy and clumsy instrument, the exact opposite of the eye. And cutting is responsible for the illusion of "looking," for restitution of the eye's immobility. Furthermore, the frame is a completely arbitrary spatial definition, as arbitrary as the stage. The absence of cutting will in the first instant reintroduce this artifice into the scene. Even if the shot-sequence restores real time and better surrounds the real space of the scene—and should therefore in principle be "truer"—the play of the camera, trapped by its continuity and incapable thenceforth of "playing the eye," distances us as much and even more.

Two other points following from that: the shot-sequence in *Jonah* doesn't play upon the time of realism (dead time, actors stammering) but upon the unity of the scene, discourse conceived each time as a little theatrical act. Henceforth, all the more because of its "natural infirmity," the camera is party to the game, an autonomous character functioning and moving according to laws that differ from those of the visible characters, staying in place when an actor changes place, leaving ahead of him or stirring when he sits down. It often happens that I will decide the path of the camera before everything else and will then set the shot—and the characters—according to this trajectory. The technique, in fact its principal agency, thus causes a return into the scene by rejecting the codes, the subjectivism of field-reverse field. By "aiming into the void," you are thus equally obliged to film the scruff of the actors' necks while "rubbing the spectator's eyes." Through reestablishing it in its true nature, the camera becomes the main transgressor of the established codes.

The shot-sequence forcefully brings back to the filming a truth clearly visible in the end-product: the truth of the working, a working neither synthesized nor fragmented, the working of the technique and the actors. The shot-sequence is a unit of work, a block containing the risk with no possibility of patching, undisguised. Here no hour of lighting set-ups intervenes between one character's question and another's reply. Here you don't hide behind splicing shots from four days ago. Obviously the shot-sequence is strictly tied to its synchronous sound (voice united with body). J.M. Straub has spoken of the difficulty of "using the scissors" when you shoot in synchronous sound. I experience the same feeling. The actors and the technicians are stimulated and inspired differently. Film a little short in the morning, another in the afternoon.

c) In *Jonah* the shot-sequence is a formal system, a little mechanical it's true, but necessary from that moment when it becomes the pivot of the discourse. Obviously it fits the epic structure (in the Brechtian sense) of the film, a sequence of scenes closed in on themselves in order the better to reply to each other. Better to isolate the elements so as to create connections among them. The unity of the shot-sequence makes it easier to detach the links of the chain.

d) The shot-sequnce privileges this supreme moment in the scene and in the shot (insofar as there are few): the cut, the transition, that 24th of a second so charged with meaning.

e) The cutting sewn in with the "invisible" montage creates the reflection of the real, the illusion, the lie. The reflection of the reflection of the real—this is what one must work toward.

f) A producer friend, a friend but a producer all the same, said to me one day, "The shot sequence is a damn nuisance." That's a good sign.

g) No, I'm not a fetishist. You can of course cut, but only in some other service to montage than simply a sewing operation. You can film in dubbed sound, but only if the choice derives from an a priori aesthetic (Bresson) and not simply from economic laziness.

Cahiers: It's very baffling, the way you systematically thwart all voyeurism, all erotic representation, in your film. As if physical relations, in this "New World of Love," only occurred in discourse ("I unbutton you . . . You unbutton me . . . ." Cut!) What did you have in mind by always cutting "at the very moment"?

A. Tanner: To thwart voyeurism, yes of course. And then what beyond that? Voyeurism has been institutionalized in cinema (X-rated) in order to obstruct the way toward all erotic representation which from that point on is segregated and associated with idiocy and ugliness. How to proceed from that point? Make real X-rated films? Perhaps. For the moment, in non-X-rated theaters, when people eat on screen they eat. When they make love on screen they pretend to. You necessarily stop at some point, generally on the verge of the ridiculous. Might as well stop earlier. And by stopping earlier you signify or mark, for want of something better, the cultural corruption which rules in this domain. This passivity weighs heavily, but I also sometimes ask myself whether sexuality, because it's such a subjective and profound experience, can really be expressed—shown—on the screen. The spoken remains, sometimes more violent and beautiful than the shown.

Cahiers: One also has the impression of rediscovering characters from your other films in *Jonah*: *Jonah* as a synthesis (apogee . . . ?) of your work. Is that intended? Do you have other projects, other films in mind? Related to the preceding ones or in some other direction?

A. Tanner: Jonah is certainly the end of something as well as the synthesis of my other films. I have the feeling of knowing a bit how to manipulate the characters of what I call my "little Geneva theater," and that I must look elsewhere (not necessarily geographically). I am beginning to mistrust humor, that double-edged weapon which turns against you, and I know that one can't walk a straight line for too long. At least to decide in which direction, even if it means stumbling one of these days. I do have certain desires in film which are quite precise regarding "how" but whose themes are still vague. Better to film facts, things, the *gestus*, and to film ideas less. Maybe it's so long for a while to that little "cafe theater" idea.

Cahiers: One gets the impression that the men in your film define themselves above all by their social position (Max ex-militant journalist, Mathieu "who belongs to the working class," Marco the teacher, Marcel the farmer-artist — the Mailman Cheval of ecology). Women on the other hand function more as "psychological" archetypes: Mathilde the mother in bloom, Marie the little girl, Madeleine the mystical vamp, and Marguerite the man-woman (who drives the tractor, keeps the books, hires the workers then entices them between the carrots and the soup). Is this why the

171

women are in part missing (that they're fantasized), and is there any way to avoid all those pigeon-holes? And how do you situate feminism among the movements we were just talking about which issued from '68? Can you talk about this, as both man and filmmaker if you like?

A. Tanner: The respective positions of the men and the women in *Jonah* correspond largely to what is still the reality within the circle, even at the margin. The wish not to stray too far from this, to avoid an avant-garde discourse, corresponded with our desire to "normalize" marginality and cause it as much as possible to reenter the circle. It's possible that the women paid for that. When I presented the film in the United States, women certainly let me know. And I think to some extent they were right; something is missing in that regard. To clear myself a little, I'll say that my two preceding films centered on the feminist discourse. It remains that on this subject men stop at some point and that only women can go on.

Cahiers: You spoke of "optimism" in regard to your film (of optimism and lucidity). Couldn't it be that it engenders a desire for practice more than a desire for discourse? (Do you sometimes manage to put yourself in the spectator's place?)

A. Tanner: Yes, I hope so. The discourse is in the body of the film. Its logical continuation in the mind of the spectator should be a desire for practice. And the operation of the film itself upon the spectator, the possibility he should have of passing through snares, through frustrations, of taking flight a bit and always landing on his feet, of believing in it and not believing. All that should question him rather than provoking the eternal *processus*: entrapment — liberation — expulsion. I always try to put myself in the spectator's place, that's obvious. You make images, sounds, and that always does something to the spectator. To ask yourself what that does is the least of it. You can also film the inside of your skull, and if you have talent that will bear witness to it, too, but I don't have the impression that I'm gifted at that.

Optimism? I've talked about it because journalists always ask me the question, as if they wanted to know whether they should be optimistic or pessimistic in their lives and in looking at world affairs. A many-sided question. Let's say that the film offers other images, other words and other heads than are found on the corpse of bourgeois representation. And eight positive heroes, all of whom "succeed in their lives," doesn't that suffice for them? To be serious, let's say that *Jonah* also contains the element of doubt, and that some have seen the slender but unyielding thread of despair running through it in places. Possible.

Cahiers: One should be able to explain this desire for practice in part by the fact that the life-styles presented there directly challenge us (us — that is the survivors of '68, of the shipwreck which capsized *Jonah* — but into what whale's belly?). Challenge in relation to a daily life (at once real and fantastical, the whole film plays on this ambiguity) whose on-screen representation allows for taking control of desire. Thus the difficulty of sustaining a critical discourse about the film (it's been impossible for me to construct a "serious" text from it — and this is where the interest in these questions comes in). But what position do you take regarding a discourse about the film? How would you like to discuss it and hear it discussed?

A. Tanner: I hoped that these life-styles presented on-screen would above all challenge others rather than those you call "the survivors of '68, the survivors of the shipwreck." First there wasn't any shipwreck, in any case not for those who, as here, were not directly acting·in the play. Because '68 (or rather May '68) was an enormous street theater with the service personnel on strike waiting for it to happen. And much more important than "the events" are the cast-offs exactly insofar as this theater brought out hopes and caused hidden desires to flower which have remained on the surface ever since. And that's what it's about, rather than the fate of the "shipwrecked." Maybe from that stems a primary difficulty.

Next, as has been noticed, *Jonah* is a film that's "double," a "double game." As you've said, the current has split into two branches in order to get through: the real (soup, work, school, children) and the fantastic. It was a difficult, precarious game, and the ambiguity flowing from it is unquestionable. Without being able to define exactly the reason for this attitude, it seemed to me impossible to attack head-on, to grapple with the subject through realistic writing, the "first level." Right off the distributors didn't know which end to grab this "product" by, what case to display it in, how to sell it. As for criticism's problems, I can't reply to them. Regarding the discourse about the film, I can only listen when it's worth the trouble (not often), or hope for some kind of echo. The film is my position. The film is something complete, but I can't foresee all the consequences concerning it. Inevitably in another's eye it's a little different than the way I made it. It exists too through what escapes me and therefore through what can reveal things to me. That is where I'm happy to listen. But listen to what? Political discourse? The official report on "the state of things"? Godard once said, "A man on horseback in a film is not a man on horseback, it's the image of a man on horseback." So when Mathieu is on his motorbike, for me it's the image of Mathieu (also it's Rufus with my raincoat, an assistant's hat and the muffler in the script). So it's the image of Mathieu that we've made with Rufus. And how does this image work, what does it tell, what does it do to the spectator? Content-oriented criticism, the practices of the characters, sure, that's obvious. But also the "practice" of expressing these other "practices." Film — and in what context, along what paths.

(Reply from Geneva to questions written in Paris by N. Heinic.

Cahiers du cinéma, n. 273, Jan.–Feb. 1977)